T&P BOOKS

DICTIONARY
THEME-BASED

British English Collection

ENGLISH-
HINDI

The most useful words
To expand your lexicon and sharpen
your language skills

3000 words

Theme-based dictionary British English-Hindi - 3000 words
By Andrey Taranov

T&P Books vocabularies are intended for helping you learn, memorize and review foreign words. The dictionary is divided into themes, covering all major spheres of everyday activities, business, science, culture, etc.

The process of learning words using T&P Books' theme-based dictionaries gives you the following advantages:

- Correctly grouped source information predetermines success at subsequent stages of word memorization
- Availability of words derived from the same root allowing memorization of word units (rather than separate words)
- Small units of words facilitate the process of establishing associative links needed for consolidation of vocabulary
- Level of language knowledge can be estimated by the number of learned words

T&P Books Publishing
www.tpbooks.com

This book is also available in E-book formats.
Please visit www.tpbooks.com or the major online bookstores.

HINDI THEME-BASED DICTIONARY
British English collection

T&P Books vocabularies are intended to help you learn, memorize, and review foreign words. The vocabulary contains over 3000 commonly used words arranged thematically.

- Vocabulary contains the most commonly used words
- Recommended as an addition to any language course
- Meets the needs of beginners and advanced learners of foreign languages
- Convenient for daily use, revision sessions, and self-testing activities
- Allows you to assess your vocabulary

Special features of the vocabulary

- Words are organized according to their meaning, not alphabetically
- Words are presented in three columns to facilitate the reviewing and self-testing processes
- Words in groups are divided into small blocks to facilitate the learning process
- The vocabulary offers a convenient and simple transcription of each foreign word

The vocabulary has 101 topics including:

Basic Concepts, Numbers, Colors, Months, Seasons, Units of Measurement, Clothing & Accessories, Food & Nutrition, Restaurant, Family Members, Relatives, Character, Feelings, Emotions, Diseases, City, Town, Sightseeing, Shopping, Money, House, Home, Office, Working in the Office, Import & Export, Marketing, Job Search, Sports, Education, Computer, Internet, Tools, Nature, Countries, Nationalities and more ...

TABLE OF CONTENTS

PRONUNCIATION GUIDE

Letter	Hindi example	T&P phonetic alphabet	English example

Vowels

अ	अक्सर	[a]; [ɑ], [ə]	park; teacher
आ	आगमन	[aː]	calf, palm
इ	इनाम	[i]	shorter than in 'feet'
ई	ईश्वर	[i], [iː]	feet, Peter
उ	उठना	[ʊ]	good, booklet
ऊ	ऊपर	[uː]	pool, room
ऋ	ऋग्वेद	[r, rʲ]	green
ए	एकता	[eː]	longer than in bell
ऐ	ऐनक	[aj]	time, white
ओ	ओला	[oː]	fall, bomb
औ	औरत	[au]	loud, powder
अं	अंजीर	[n]	English, ring
अः	अ से अः	[h]	home, have
ऑ	ऑफिस	[ɒ]	cotton, pocket

Consonants

क	कमरा	[k]	clock, kiss
ख	खिड़की	[kh]	work hard
ग	गरज	[g]	game, gold
घ	घर	[gh]	g aspirated
ङ	डाकू	[n]	English, ring
च	चक्कर	[ʧ]	church, French
छ	छात्र	[ʧh]	hitchhiker
ज	जाना	[ʤ]	joke, general
झ	झलक	[ʤ]	joke, general
ञ	विज्ञान	[n]	canyon, new
ट	मटर	[t]	tourist, trip
ठ	ठेका	[th]	don't have
ड	डंडा	[d]	day, doctor
ढ	ढलान	[d]	day, doctor
ण	क्षण	[n]	retroflex nasal
त	ताकत	[t]	tourist, trip
थ	थकना	[th]	don't have
द	दरवाज़ा	[d]	day, doctor
ध	धोना	[d]	day, doctor
न	नाई	[n]	sang, thing

Letter	Hindi example	T&P phonetic alphabet	English example
प	पिता	[p]	pencil, private
फ	फल	[f]	face, food
ब	बच्चा	[b]	baby, book
भ	भाई	[b]	baby, book
म	माता	[m]	magic, milk
य	याद	[j]	yes, New York
र	रीछ	[r]	rice, radio
ल	लाल	[l]	lace, people
व	वचन	[v]	very, river
श	शिक्षक	[ʃ]	machine, shark
ष	भाषा	[ʃ]	machine, shark
स	सोना	[s]	city, boss
ह	हज़ार	[h]	home, have

Additional consonants

Letter	Hindi example	T&P phonetic alphabet	English example
क़	क़लम	[q]	king, club
ख़	ख़बर	[h]	huge, hat
ड़	लड़का	[r]	rice, radio
ढ़	पढ़ना	[r]	rice, radio
ग़	ग़लती	[ɣ]	between [g] and [h]
ज़	ज़िन्दगी	[z]	zebra, please
झ़	टैंझर	[ʒ]	forge, pleasure
फ़	फ़ौज	[f]	face, food

ABBREVIATIONS
used in the dictionary

English abbreviations

ab.	-	about
adj	-	adjective
adv	-	adverb
anim.	-	animate
as adj	-	attributive noun used as adjective
e.g.	-	for example
etc.	-	et cetera
fam.	-	familiar
fem.	-	feminine
form.	-	formal
inanim.	-	inanimate
masc.	-	masculine
math	-	mathematics
mil.	-	military
n	-	noun
pl	-	plural
pron.	-	pronoun
sb	-	somebody
sing.	-	singular
sth	-	something
v aux	-	auxiliary verb
vi	-	intransitive verb
vi, vt	-	intransitive, transitive verb
vt	-	transitive verb

Hindi abbreviations

f	-	feminine noun
f pl	-	feminine plural
m	-	masculine noun
m pl	-	masculine plural

BASIC CONCEPTS

1. Pronouns

I, me	मैं	main
you	तुम	tum
he, she, it	वह	vah
we	हम	ham
you (to a group)	आप	āp
they	वे	ve

2. Greetings. Salutations

Hello! (fam.)	नमस्कार!	namaskār!
Hello! (form.)	नमस्ते!	namaste!
Good morning!	नमस्ते!	namaste!
Good afternoon!	नमस्ते!	namaste!
Good evening!	नमस्ते!	namaste!
to say hello	नमस्कार कहना	namaskār kahana
Hi! (hello)	नमस्कार!	namaskār!
greeting (n)	अभिवादन (m)	abhivādan
to greet (vt)	अभिवादन करना	abhivādan karana
How are you?	आप कैसे हैं?	āp kaise hain?
What's new?	क्या हाल है?	kya hāl hai?
Bye-Bye! Goodbye!	अलविदा!	alavida!
See you soon!	फिर मिलेंगे!	fir milenge!
Farewell! (to a friend)	अलिवदा!	alivada!
Farewell! (form.)	अलविदा!	alavida!
to say goodbye	अलविदा कहना	alavida kahana
Cheers!	अलविदा!	alavida!
Thank you! Cheers!	धन्यवाद!	dhanyavād!
Thank you very much!	बहुत बहुत शुक्रिया!	bahut bahut shukriya!
My pleasure!	कोई बात नहीं	koī bāt nahin
Don't mention it!	कोई बात नहीं	koī bāt nahin
It was nothing	कोई बात नहीं	koī bāt nahin
Excuse me! (fam.)	माफ़ कीजिएगा!	māf kījiega!
Excuse me! (form.)	माफ़ी कीजियेगा!	māfī kījiyega!
to excuse (forgive)	माफ़ करना	māf karana
to apologize (vi)	माफ़ी मांगना	māfī māngana
My apologies	मुझे माफ़ कीजिएगा	mujhe māf kījiega
I'm sorry!	मुझे माफ़ कीजिएगा!	mujhe māf kījiega!
to forgive (vt)	माफ़ करना	māf karana

please (adv)	कृप्या	krpya
Don't forget!	भूलना नहीं!	bhūlana nahin!
Certainly!	ज़रूर!	zarūr!
Of course not!	बिल्कुल नहीं!	bilkul nahin!
Okay! (I agree)	ठीक है!	thīk hai!
That's enough!	बहुत हुआ!	bahut hua!

3. Questions

Who?	कौन?	kaun?
What?	क्या?	kya?
Where? (at, in)	कहाँ?	kahān?
Where (to)?	किधर?	kidhar?
From where?	कहाँ से?	kahān se?
When?	कब?	kab?
Why? (What for?)	क्यों?	kyon?
Why? (~ are you crying?)	क्यों?	kyon?
What for?	किस लिये?	kis liye?
How? (in what way)	कैसे?	kaise?
What? (What kind of ...?)	कौन-सा?	kaun-sa?
Which?	कौन-सा?	kaun-sa?
To whom?	किसको?	kisako?
About whom?	किसके बारे में?	kisake bāre men?
About what?	किसके बारे में?	kisake bāre men?
With whom?	किसके?	kisake?
How many? How much?	कितना?	kitana?
Whose?	किसका?	kisaka?

4. Prepositions

with (accompanied by)	के साथ	ke sāth
without	के बिना	ke bina
to (indicating direction)	की तरफ़	kī taraf
about (talking ~ ...)	के बारे में	ke bāre men
before (in time)	के पहले	ke pahale
in front of ...	के सामने	ke sāmane
under (beneath, below)	के नीचे	ke nīche
above (over)	के ऊपर	ke ūpar
on (atop)	पर	par
from (off, out of)	से	se
of (made from)	से	se
in (e.g. ~ ten minutes)	में	men
over (across the top of)	के ऊपर चढ़कर	ke ūpar charhakar

5. Function words. Adverbs. Part 1

Where? (at, in)	कहाँ?	kahān?
here (adv)	यहाँ	yahān
there (adv)	वहां	vahān
somewhere (to be)	कहीं	kahīn
nowhere (not in any place)	कहीं नहीं	kahīn nahin
by (near, beside)	के पास	ke pās
by the window	खिड़की के पास	khirakī ke pās
Where (to)?	किधर?	kidhar?
here (e.g. come ~!)	इधर	idhar
there (e.g. to go ~)	उधर	udhar
from here (adv)	यहां से	yahān se
from there (adv)	वहां से	vahān se
close (adv)	पास	pās
far (adv)	दूर	dūr
near (e.g. ~ Paris)	निकट	nikat
nearby (adv)	पास	pās
not far (adv)	दूर नहीं	dūr nahin
left (adj)	बायाँ	bāyān
on the left	बायीं तरफ़	bāyīn taraf
to the left	बायीं तरफ़	bāyīn taraf
right (adj)	दायां	dāyān
on the right	दायीं तरफ़	dāyīn taraf
to the right	दायीं तरफ़	dāyīn taraf
in front (adv)	सामने	sāmane
front (as adj)	सामने का	sāmane ka
ahead (the kids ran ~)	आगे	āge
behind (adv)	पीछे	pīchhe
from behind	पीछे से	pīchhe se
back (towards the rear)	पीछे	pīchhe
middle	बीच (m)	bīch
in the middle	बीच में	bīch men
at the side	कोने में	kone men
everywhere (adv)	सभी	sabhī
around (in all directions)	आस-पास	ās-pās
from inside	अंदर से	andar se
somewhere (to go)	कहीं	kahīn
straight (directly)	सीधे	sīdhe
back (e.g. come ~)	वापस	vāpas
from anywhere	कहीं से भी	kahīn se bhī
from somewhere	कहीं से	kahīn se

firstly (adv)	पहले	pahale
secondly (adv)	दूसरा	dūsara
thirdly (adv)	तीसरा	tīsara

suddenly (adv)	अचानक	achānak
at first (in the beginning)	शुरू में	shurū men
for the first time	पहली बार	pahalī bār
long before ...	बहुत समय पहले ...	bahut samay pahale ...
anew (over again)	नई शुरूआत	naī shurūāt
for good (adv)	हमेशा के लिए	hamesha ke lie

never (adv)	कभी नहीं	kabhī nahin
again (adv)	फिर से	fir se
now (at present)	अब	ab
often (adv)	अकसर	akasar
then (adv)	तब	tab
urgently (quickly)	तत्काल	tatkāl
usually (adv)	आमतौर पर	āmataur par

by the way, ...	प्रसंगवश	prasangavash
possibly	मुमकिन	mumakin
probably (adv)	संभव	sambhav
maybe (adv)	शायद	shāyad
besides ...	इस के अलावा	is ke alāva
that's why ...	इस लिए	is lie
in spite of ...	फिर भी ...	fir bhī ...
thanks to ...	... की मेहरबानी से	... kī meharabānī se

what (pron.)	क्या	kya
that (conj.)	कि	ki
something	कुछ	kuchh
anything (something)	कुछ भी	kuchh bhī
nothing	कुछ नहीं	kuchh nahin

who (pron.)	कौन	kaun
someone	कोई	koī
somebody	कोई	koī

nobody	कोई नहीं	koī nahin
nowhere (a voyage to ~)	कहीं नहीं	kahīn nahin
nobody's	किसी का नहीं	kisī ka nahin
somebody's	किसी का	kisī ka

so (I'm ~ glad)	कितना	kitana
also (as well)	भी	bhī
too (as well)	भी	bhī

6. Function words. Adverbs. Part 2

Why?	क्यों?	kyon?
for some reason	किसी कारणवश	kisī kāranavash
because ...	क्यों कि ...	kyon ki ...
for some purpose	किसी वजह से	kisī vajah se
and	और	aur

or	या	ya
but	लेकिन	lekin
for (e.g. ~ me)	के लिए	ke lie
too (excessively)	ज़्यादा	zyāda
only (exclusively)	सिर्फ़	sirf
exactly (adv)	ठीक	thīk
about (more or less)	करीब	karīb
approximately (adv)	लगभग	lagabhag
approximate (adj)	अनुमानित	anumānit
almost (adv)	करीब	karīb
the rest	बाक़ी	bāqī
each (adj)	हर एक	har ek
any (no matter which)	कोई	koī
many, much (a lot of)	बहुत	bahut
many people	बहुत लोग	bahut log
all (everyone)	सभी	sabhī
in return for ...	... के बदले में	... ke badale men
in exchange (adv)	की जगह	kī jagah
by hand (made)	हाथ से	hāth se
hardly (negative opinion)	शायद ही	shāyad hī
probably (adv)	शायद	shāyad
on purpose (intentionally)	जानबूझकर	jānabūjhakar
by accident (adv)	संयोगवश	sanyogavash
very (adv)	बहुत	bahut
for example (adv)	उदाहरण के लिए	udāharan ke lie
between	के बीच	ke bīch
among	में	men
so much (such a lot)	इतना	itana
especially (adv)	ख़ासतौर पर	khāsataur par

NUMBERS. MISCELLANEOUS

7. Cardinal numbers. Part 1

0 zero	ज़ीरो	zīro
1 one	एक	ek
2 two	दो	do
3 three	तीन	tīn
4 four	चार	chār
5 five	पाँच	pānch
6 six	छह	chhah
7 seven	सात	sāt
8 eight	आठ	āth
9 nine	नौ	nau
10 ten	दस	das
11 eleven	ग्यारह	gyārah
12 twelve	बारह	bārah
13 thirteen	तेरह	terah
14 fourteen	चौदह	chaudah
15 fifteen	पन्द्रह	pandrah
16 sixteen	सोलह	solah
17 seventeen	सत्रह	satrah
18 eighteen	अठारह	athārah
19 nineteen	उन्नीस	unnīs
20 twenty	बीस	bīs
21 twenty-one	इक्कीस	ikkīs
22 twenty-two	बाईस	baīs
23 twenty-three	तेईस	teīs
30 thirty	तीस	tīs
31 thirty-one	इकत्तीस	ikattīs
32 thirty-two	बत्तीस	battīs
33 thirty-three	तैंतीस	taintīs
40 forty	चालीस	chālīs
41 forty-one	इक्तालीस	iktālīs
42 forty-two	बयालीस	bayālīs
43 forty-three	तैंतालीस	taintālīs
50 fifty	पचास	pachās
51 fifty-one	इक्यावन	ikyāvan
52 fifty-two	बावन	bāvan
53 fifty-three	तिरपन	tirapan
60 sixty	साठ	sāth
61 sixty-one	इकसठ	ikasath

62 sixty-two	बासठ	bāsaṭh
63 sixty-three	तिरसठ	tirasaṭh
70 seventy	सत्तर	sattar
71 seventy-one	इकहत्तर	ikahattar
72 seventy-two	बहत्तर	bahattar
73 seventy-three	तिहत्तर	tihattar
80 eighty	अस्सी	assī
81 eighty-one	इक्यासी	ikyāsī
82 eighty-two	बयासी	bayāsī
83 eighty-three	तिरासी	tirāsī
90 ninety	नब्बे	nabbe
91 ninety-one	इक्यानवे	ikyānave
92 ninety-two	बानवे	bānave
93 ninety-three	तिरानवे	tirānave

8. Cardinal numbers. Part 2

100 one hundred	सौ	sau
200 two hundred	दो सौ	do sau
300 three hundred	तीन सौ	tīn sau
400 four hundred	चार सौ	chār sau
500 five hundred	पाँच सौ	pānch sau
600 six hundred	छह सौ	chhah sau
700 seven hundred	सात सो	sāt so
800 eight hundred	आठ सौ	āṭh sau
900 nine hundred	नौ सौ	nau sau
1000 one thousand	एक हज़ार	ek hazār
2000 two thousand	दो हज़ार	do hazār
3000 three thousand	तीन हज़ार	tīn hazār
10000 ten thousand	दस हज़ार	das hazār
one hundred thousand	एक लाख	ek lākh
million	दस लाख (m)	das lākh
billion	अरब (m)	arab

9. Ordinal numbers

first (adj)	पहला	pahala
second (adj)	दूसरा	dūsara
third (adj)	तीसरा	tīsara
fourth (adj)	चौथा	chautha
fifth (adj)	पाँचवाँ	pānchavān
sixth (adj)	छठा	chhatha
seventh (adj)	सातवाँ	sātavān
eighth (adj)	आठवाँ	āthavān
ninth (adj)	नौवाँ	nauvān
tenth (adj)	दसवाँ	dasavān

COLORS. UNITS OF MEASUREMENT

10. Colours

colour	रंग (m)	rang
shade (tint)	रंग (m)	rang
hue	रंग (m)	rang
rainbow	इन्द्रधनुष (f)	indradhanush
white (adj)	सफ़ेद	safed
black (adj)	काला	kāla
grey (adj)	धूसर	dhūsar
green (adj)	हरा	hara
yellow (adj)	पीला	pīla
red (adj)	लाल	lāl
blue (adj)	नीला	nīla
light blue (adj)	हल्का नीला	halka nīla
pink (adj)	गुलाबी	gulābī
orange (adj)	नारंगी	nārangī
violet (adj)	बैंगनी	bainganī
brown (adj)	भूरा	bhūra
golden (adj)	सुनहरा	sunahara
silvery (adj)	चांदी-जैसा	chāndī-jaisa
beige (adj)	हल्का भूरा	halka bhūra
cream (adj)	क्रीम	krīm
turquoise (adj)	फ़ीरोज़ी	fīrozī
cherry red (adj)	चेरी जैसा लाल	cherī jaisa lāl
lilac (adj)	हल्का बैंगनी	halka bainganī
crimson (adj)	गहरा लाल	gahara lāl
light (adj)	हल्का	halka
dark (adj)	गहरा	gahara
bright, vivid (adj)	चमकीला	chamakīla
coloured (pencils)	रंगीन	rangīn
colour (e.g. ~ film)	रंगीन	rangīn
black-and-white (adj)	काला-सफ़ेद	kāla-safed
plain (one-coloured)	एक रंग का	ek rang ka
multicoloured (adj)	बहुरंगी	bahurangī

11. Units of measurement

weight	वज़न (m)	vazan
length	लम्बाई (f)	lambaī

width	चौड़ाई (f)	chauraī
height	ऊंचाई (f)	ūnchaī
depth	गहराई (f)	gaharaī
volume	घनत्व (f)	ghanatv
area	क्षेत्रफल (m)	kshetrafal

gram	ग्राम (m)	grām
milligram	मिलीग्राम (m)	milīgrām
kilogram	किलोग्राम (m)	kilogrām
ton	टन (m)	tan
pound	पौण्ड (m)	paund
ounce	औन्स (m)	auns

metre	मीटर (m)	mītar
millimetre	मिलीमीटर (m)	milīmītar
centimetre	सेंटीमीटर (m)	sentīmītar
kilometre	किलोमीटर (m)	kilomītar
mile	मील (m)	mīl

inch	इंच (m)	inch
foot	फुट (m)	fut
yard	गज (m)	gaj

| square metre | वर्ग मीटर (m) | varg mītar |
| hectare | हेक्टेयर (m) | hekteyar |

litre	लीटर (m)	lītar
degree	डिग्री (m)	digrī
volt	वोल्ट (m)	volt
ampere	ऐम्पेयर (m)	aimpeyar
horsepower	अश्व शक्ति (f)	ashv shakti

quantity	मात्रा (f)	mātra
a little bit of ...	कुछ ...	kuchh ...
half	आधा (m)	ādha
dozen	दर्जन (m)	darjan
piece (item)	टुकड़ा (m)	tukara

| size | माप (m) | māp |
| scale (map ~) | पैमाना (m) | paimāna |

minimal (adj)	न्यूनतम	nyūnatam
the smallest (adj)	सब से छोटा	sab se chhota
medium (adj)	मध्य	madhy
maximal (adj)	अधिकतम	adhikatam
the largest (adj)	सबसे बड़ा	sabase bara

12. Containers

canning jar (glass ~)	शीशी (f)	shīshī
tin, can	डिब्बा (m)	dibba
bucket	बाल्टी (f)	bāltī
barrel	पीपा (m)	pīpa
wash basin (e.g., plastic ~)	चिलमची (f)	chilamachī

tank (100L water ~)	कुण्ड (m)	kund
hip flask	फ्लास्क (m)	flāsk
jerrycan	जेरिकैन (m)	jerikain
tank (e.g., tank car)	टंकी (f)	tankī
mug	मग (m)	mag
cup (of coffee, etc.)	प्याली (f)	pyālī
saucer	सॉसर (m)	sosar
glass (tumbler)	गिलास (m)	gilās
wine glass	वाइन गिलास (m)	vain gilās
stock pot (soup pot)	सॉसपैन (m)	sosapain
bottle (~ of wine)	बोतल (f)	botal
neck (of the bottle, etc.)	गला (m)	gala
carafe (decanter)	जग (m)	jag
pitcher	सुराही (f)	surāhī
vessel (container)	बरतन (m)	baratan
pot (crock, stoneware ~)	घड़ा (m)	ghara
vase	फूलदान (m)	fūladān
flacon, bottle (perfume ~)	शीशी (f)	shīshī
vial, small bottle	शीशी (f)	shīshī
tube (of toothpaste)	ट्यूब (m)	tyūb
sack (bag)	थैला (m)	thaila
bag (paper ~, plastic ~)	थैली (f)	thailī
packet (of cigarettes, etc.)	पैकेट (f)	paiket
box (e.g. shoebox)	डिब्बा (m)	dibba
crate	डिब्बा (m)	dibba
basket	टोकरी (f)	tokarī

MAIN VERBS

13. The most important verbs. Part 1

to advise (vt)	सलाह देना	salāh dena
to agree (say yes)	राज़ी होना	rāzī hona
to answer (vi, vt)	जवाब देना	javāb dena
to apologize (vi)	माफ़ी मांगना	māfī māngana
to arrive (vi)	पहुँचना	pahunchana
to ask (~ oneself)	पूछना	pūchhana
to ask (~ sb to do sth)	मांगना	māngana
to be (vi)	होना	hona
to be afraid	डरना	darana
to be hungry	भूख लगना	bhūkh lagana
to be interested in …	रुचि लेना	ruchi lena
to be needed	आवश्यक होना	āvashyak hona
to be surprised	हैरान होना	hairān hona
to be thirsty	प्यास लगना	pyās lagana
to begin (vt)	शुरू करना	shurū karana
to belong to …	स्वामी होना	svāmī hona
to boast (vi)	डींग मारना	dīng mārana
to break (split into pieces)	तोड़ना	torana
to call (~ for help)	बुलाना	bulāna
can (v aux)	सकना	sakana
to catch (vt)	पकड़ना	pakarana
to change (vt)	बदलना	badalana
to choose (select)	चुनना	chunana
to come down (the stairs)	उतरना	utarana
to compare (vt)	तुलना करना	tulana karana
to complain (vi, vt)	शिकायत करना	shikāyat karana
to confuse (mix up)	गड़बड़ा जाना	garabara jāna
to continue (vt)	जारी रखना	jārī rakhana
to control (vt)	नियंत्रित करना	niyantrit karana
to cook (dinner)	खाना बनाना	khāna banāna
to cost (vt)	दाम होना	dām hona
to count (add up)	गिनना	ginana
to count on …	भरोसा रखना	bharosa rakhana
to create (vt)	बनाना	banāna
to cry (weep)	रोना	rona

14. The most important verbs. Part 2

to deceive (vi, vt)	धोखा देना	dhokha dena
to decorate (tree, street)	सजाना	sajāna

to defend (a country, etc.)	रक्षा करना	raksha karana
to demand (request firmly)	माँगना	māngana
to dig (vt)	खोदना	khodana
to discuss (vt)	चर्चा करना	charcha karana
to do (vt)	करना	karana
to doubt (have doubts)	शक करना	shak karana
to drop (let fall)	गिराना	girāna
to enter (room, house, etc.)	अंदर आना	andar āna
to exist (vi)	होना	hona
to expect (foresee)	उम्मीद करना	ummīd karana
to explain (vt)	समझाना	samajhāna
to fall (vi)	गिरना	girana
to fancy (vt)	पसंद करना	pasand karana
to find (vt)	ढूढ़ना	dhūrhana
to finish (vt)	ख़त्म करना	khatm karana
to fly (vi)	उड़ना	urana
to follow ... (come after)	पीछे चलना	pīchhe chalana
to forget (vi, vt)	भूलना	bhūlana
to forgive (vt)	क्षमा करना	kshama karana
to give (vt)	देना	dena
to give a hint	इशारा करना	ishāra karana
to go (on foot)	जाना	jāna
to go for a swim	तैरना	tairana
to go out (for dinner, etc.)	बाहर जाना	bāhar jāna
to guess (the answer)	अंदाज़ा लगाना	andāza lagāna
to have (vt)	होना	hona
to have breakfast	नाश्ता करना	nāshta karana
to have dinner	रात्रिभोज करना	rātribhoj karana
to have lunch	दोपहर का भोजन करना	dopahar ka bhojan karana
to hear (vt)	सुनना	sunana
to help (vt)	मदद करना	madad karana
to hide (vt)	छिपाना	chhipāna
to hope (vi, vt)	आशा करना	āsha karana
to hunt (vi, vt)	शिकार करना	shikār karana
to hurry (vi)	जल्दी करना	jaldī karana

15. The most important verbs. Part 3

to inform (vt)	खबर देना	khabar dena
to insist (vi, vt)	आग्रह करना	āgrah karana
to insult (vt)	अपमान करना	apamān karana
to invite (vt)	आमंत्रित करना	āmantrit karana
to joke (vi)	मज़ाक करना	mazāk karana
to keep (vt)	रखना	rakhana
to keep silent, to hush	चुप रहना	chup rahana
to kill (vt)	मार डालना	mār dālana

to know (sb)	जानना	jānana
to know (sth)	मालूम होना	mālūm hona
to laugh (vi)	हंसना	hansana
to liberate (city, etc.)	आज़ाद करना	āzād karana
to look for … (search)	तलाश करना	talāsh karana
to love (sb)	प्यार करना	pyār karana
to make a mistake	गलती करना	galatī karana
to manage, to run	प्रबंधन करना	prabandhan karana
to mean (signify)	अर्थ होना	arth hona
to mention (talk about)	उल्लेख करना	ullekh karana
to miss (school, etc.)	ग़ैर-हाज़िर होना	gair-hāzir hona
to notice (see)	देखना	dekhana
to object (vi, vt)	एतराज़ करना	etarāz karana
to observe (see)	देखना	dekhana
to open (vt)	खोलना	kholana
to order (meal, etc.)	ऑर्डर करना	ordar karana
to order (mil.)	हुक्म देना	hukm dena
to own (possess)	मालिक होना	mālik hona
to participate (vi)	भाग लेना	bhāg lena
to pay (vi, vt)	दाम चुकाना	dām chukāna
to permit (vt)	अनुमति देना	anumati dena
to plan (vt)	योजना बनाना	yojana banāna
to play (children)	खेलना	khelana
to pray (vi, vt)	दुआ देना	dua dena
to prefer (vt)	तरजीह देना	tarajīh dena
to promise (vt)	वचन देना	vachan dena
to pronounce (vt)	उच्चारण करना	uchchāran karana
to propose (vt)	प्रस्ताव रखना	prastāv rakhana
to punish (vt)	सज़ा देना	saza dena

16. The most important verbs. Part 4

to read (vi, vt)	पढ़ना	parhana
to recommend (vt)	सिफ़ारिश करना	sifārish karana
to refuse (vi, vt)	इन्कार करना	inkār karana
to regret (be sorry)	अफ़सोस जताना	afasos jatāna
to rent (sth from sb)	किराए पर लेना	kirae par lena
to repeat (say again)	दोहराना	doharāna
to reserve, to book	बुक करना	buk karana
to run (vi)	दौड़ना	daurana
to save (rescue)	बचाना	bachāna
to say (~ thank you)	कहना	kahana
to scold (vt)	डाँटना	dāntana
to see (vt)	देखना	dekhana
to sell (vt)	बेचना	bechana
to send (vt)	भेजना	bhejana
to shoot (vi)	गोली चलाना	golī chalāna

to shout (vi)	चिल्लाना	chillāna
to show (vt)	दिखाना	dikhāna
to sign (document)	हस्ताक्षर करना	hastākshar karana
to sit down (vi)	बैठना	baithana
to smile (vi)	मुस्कुराना	muskurāna
to speak (vi, vt)	बोलना	bolana
to steal (money, etc.)	चुराना	churāna
to stop (for pause, etc.)	रुकना	rukana
to stop (please ~ calling me)	बंद करना	band karana
to study (vt)	पढ़ाई करना	parhaī karana
to swim (vi)	तैरना	tairana
to take (vt)	लेना	lena
to think (vi, vt)	सोचना	sochana
to threaten (vt)	धमकाना	dhamakāna
to touch (with hands)	छूना	chhūna
to translate (vt)	अनुवाद करना	anuvād karana
to trust (vt)	यकीन करना	yakīn karana
to try (attempt)	कोशिश करना	koshish karana
to turn (e.g., ~ left)	मुड़ जाना	mur jāna
to underestimate (vt)	कम मूल्यांकन करना	kam mūlyānkan karana
to understand (vt)	समझना	samajhana
to unite (vt)	संयुक्त करना	sanyukt karana
to wait (vt)	इंतज़ार करना	intazār karana
to want (wish, desire)	चाहना	chāhana
to warn (vt)	चेतावनी देना	chetāvanī dena
to work (vi)	काम करना	kām karana
to write (vt)	लिखना	likhana
to write down	लिख लेना	likh lena

TIME. CALENDAR

17. Weekdays

Monday	सोमवार (m)	somavār
Tuesday	मंगलवार (m)	mangalavār
Wednesday	बुधवार (m)	budhavār
Thursday	गुरूवार (m)	gurūvār
Friday	शुक्रवार (m)	shukravār
Saturday	शनिवार (m)	shanivār
Sunday	रविवार (m)	ravivār
today (adv)	आज	āj
tomorrow (adv)	कल	kal
the day after tomorrow	परसों	parason
yesterday (adv)	कल	kal
the day before yesterday	परसों	parason
day	दिन (m)	din
working day	कार्यदिवस (m)	kāryadivas
public holiday	सार्वजनिक छुट्टी (f)	sārvajanik chhuttī
day off	छुट्टी का दिन (m)	chhuttī ka din
weekend	सप्ताहांत (m)	saptāhānt
all day long	सारा दिन	sāra din
the next day (adv)	अगला दिन	agala din
two days ago	दो दिन पहले	do din pahale
the day before	एक दिन पहले	ek din pahale
daily (adj)	दैनिक	dainik
every day (adv)	हर दिन	har din
week	हफ़्ता (f)	hafata
last week (adv)	पिछले हफ़्ते	pichhale hafate
next week (adv)	अगले हफ़्ते	agale hafate
weekly (adj)	सप्ताहिक	saptāhik
every week (adv)	हर हफ़्ते	har hafate
twice a week	हफ़्ते में दो बार	hafate men do bār
every Tuesday	हर मंगलवार को	har mangalavār ko

18. Hours. Day and night

morning	सुबह (m)	subah
in the morning	सुबह में	subah men
noon, midday	दोपहर (m)	dopahar
in the afternoon	दोपहर में	dopahar men
evening	शाम (m)	shām
in the evening	शाम में	shām men

night	रात (f)	rāt
at night	रात में	rāt men
midnight	आधी रात (f)	ādhī rāt
second	सेकन्ड (m)	sekand
minute	मिनट (m)	minat
hour	घंटा (m)	ghanta
half an hour	आधा घंटा	ādha ghanta
a quarter-hour	सवा	sava
fifteen minutes	पंद्रह मीनट	pandrah mīnat
24 hours	24 घंटे (m)	chaubīs ghante
sunrise	सूर्योदय (m)	sūryoday
dawn	सूर्योदय (m)	sūryoday
early morning	प्रातःकाल (m)	prātahkāl
sunset	सूर्यास्त (m)	sūryāst
early in the morning	सुबह-सवेरे	subah-savere
this morning	इस सुबह	is subah
tomorrow morning	कल सुबह	kal subah
this afternoon	आज शाम	āj shām
in the afternoon	दोपहर में	dopahar men
tomorrow afternoon	कल दोपहर	kal dopahar
tonight (this evening)	आज शाम	āj shām
tomorrow night	कल रात	kal rāt
at 3 o'clock sharp	ठीक तीन बजे में	thīk tīn baje men
about 4 o'clock	लगभग चार बजे	lagabhag chār baje
by 12 o'clock	बारह बजे तक	bārah baje tak
in 20 minutes	बीस मीनट में	bīs mīnat men
in an hour	एक घंटे में	ek ghante men
on time (adv)	ठीक समय पर	thīk samay par
a quarter to ...	पौने ... बजे	paune ... baje
within an hour	एक घंटे के अंदर	ek ghante ke andar
every 15 minutes	हर पंद्रह मीनट	har pandrah mīnat
round the clock	दिन-रात (m pl)	din-rāt

19. Months. Seasons

January	जनवरी (m)	janavarī
February	फ़रवरी (m)	faravarī
March	मार्च (m)	mārch
April	अप्रैल (m)	aprail
May	माई (m)	maī
June	जून (m)	jūn
July	जुलाई (m)	julaī
August	अगस्त (m)	agast
September	सितम्बर (m)	sitambar
October	अक्तूबर (m)	aktūbar

| November | नवम्बर (m) | navambar |
| December | दिसम्बर (m) | disambar |

spring	वसन्त (m)	vasant
in spring	वसन्त में	vasant men
spring (as adj)	वसन्त	vasant

summer	गरमी (f)	garamī
in summer	गरमियों में	garamiyon men
summer (as adj)	गरमी	garamī

autumn	शरद (m)	sharad
in autumn	शरद में	sharad men
autumn (as adj)	शरद	sharad

winter	सर्दी (f)	sardī
in winter	सर्दियों में	sardiyon men
winter (as adj)	सर्दी	sardī

month	महीना (m)	mahīna
this month	इस महीने	is mahīne
next month	अगले महीने	agale mahīne
last month	पिछले महीने	pichhale mahīne

a month ago	एक महीने पहले	ek mahīne pahale
in a month (a month later)	एक महीने में	ek mahīne men
in 2 months (2 months later)	दो महीने में	do mahīne men
the whole month	पूरे महीने	pūre mahīne
all month long	पूरे महीने	pūre mahīne

monthly (~ magazine)	मासिक	māsik
monthly (adv)	हर महीने	har mahīne
every month	हर महीने	har mahīne
twice a month	महीने में दो बार	mahine men do bār

year	वर्ष (m)	varsh
this year	इस साल	is sāl
next year	अगले साल	agale sāl
last year	पिछले साल	pichhale sāl

a year ago	एक साल पहले	ek sāl pahale
in a year	एक साल में	ek sāl men
in two years	दो साल में	do sāl men
the whole year	पूरा साल	pūra sāl
all year long	पूरा साल	pūra sāl

every year	हर साल	har sāl
annual (adj)	वार्षिक	vārshik
annually (adv)	वार्षिक	vārshik
4 times a year	साल में चार बार	sāl men chār bār

date (e.g. today's ~)	तारीख़ (f)	tārīkh
date (e.g. ~ of birth)	तारीख़ (f)	tārīkh
calendar	कैलेन्डर (m)	kailendar
half a year	आधे वर्ष (m)	ādhe varsh
six months	छमाही (f)	chhamāhī

| season (summer, etc.) | मौसम (m) | mausam |
| century | शताब्दी (f) | shatābadī |

TRAVEL. HOTEL

20. Trip. Travel

tourism, travel	पर्यटन (m)	paryatan
tourist	पर्यटक (m)	paryatak
trip, voyage	यात्रा (f)	yātra
adventure	जाँबाज़ी (f)	jānbāzī
trip, journey	यात्रा (f)	yātra
holiday	छुट्टी (f)	chhuttī
to be on holiday	छुट्टी पर होना	chhuttī par hona
rest	आराम (m)	ārām
train	रेलगाड़ी, ट्रेन (f)	relagāṛī, tren
by train	रैलगाड़ी से	railagāṛī se
aeroplane	विमान (m)	vimān
by aeroplane	विमान से	vimān se
by car	कार से	kār se
by ship	जहाज़ पर	jahāz par
luggage	सामान (m)	sāmān
suitcase	सूटकेस (m)	sūtakes
luggage trolley	सामान के लिये गाड़ी (f)	sāmān ke liye gārī
passport	पासपोर्ट (m)	pāsaport
visa	वीज़ा (m)	vīza
ticket	टिकट (m)	tikat
air ticket	हवाई टिकट (m)	havaī tikat
guidebook	गाइडबुक (f)	gaidabuk
map (tourist ~)	नक्शा (m)	naksha
area (rural ~)	क्षेत्र (m)	kshetr
place, site	स्थान (m)	sthān
exotica (n)	विचित्र वस्तुएं	vichitr vastuen
exotic (adj)	विचित्र	vichitr
amazing (adj)	अजीब	ajīb
group	समूह (m)	samūh
excursion, sightseeing tour	पर्यटन (f)	paryatan
guide (person)	गाइड (m)	gaid

21. Hotel

hotel	होटल (f)	hotal
motel	मोटेल (m)	motal
three-star (~ hotel)	तीन सितारा	tīn sitāra

five-star	पाँच सितारा	pānch sitāra
to stay (in a hotel, etc.)	ठहरना	thaharana
room	कमरा (m)	kamara
single room	एक पलंग का कमरा (m)	ek palang ka kamara
double room	दो पलंगों का कमरा (m)	do palangon ka kamara
to book a room	कमरा बुक करना	kamara buk karana
half board	हाफ़-बोर्ड (m)	hāf-bord
full board	फ़ुल-बोर्ड (m)	ful-bord
with bath	स्नानघर के साथ	snānaghar ke sāth
with shower	शॉवर के साथ	shovar ke sāth
satellite television	सैटेलाइट टेलीविज़न (m)	saitelait telīvizan
air-conditioner	एयर-कंडिशनर (m)	eyar-kandishanar
towel	तौलिया (f)	tauliya
key	चाबी (f)	chābī
administrator	मैनेजर (m)	mainejar
chambermaid	चैमबरमैड (f)	chaimabaramaid
porter	कुली (m)	kulī
doorman	दरबान (m)	darabān
restaurant	रेस्टराँ (m)	restarān
pub, bar	बार (m)	bār
breakfast	नाश्ता (m)	nāshta
dinner	रात्रिभोज (m)	rātribhoj
buffet	बुफ़े (m)	bufe
lobby	लॉबी (f)	lobī
lift	लिफ़्ट (m)	lift
DO NOT DISTURB	परेशान न करें	pareshān na karen
NO SMOKING	धूम्रपान निषेध!	dhumrapān nishedh!

22. Sightseeing

monument	स्मारक (m)	smārak
fortress	किला (m)	kila
palace	भवन (m)	bhavan
castle	महल (m)	mahal
tower	मीनार (m)	mīnār
mausoleum	समाधि (f)	samādhi
architecture	वस्तुशाला (m)	vastushāla
medieval (adj)	मध्ययुगीय	madhayayugīy
ancient (adj)	प्राचीन	prāchīn
national (adj)	राष्ट्रीय	rāshtrīy
famous (monument, etc.)	मशहूर	mashhūr
tourist	पर्यटक (m)	paryatak
guide (person)	गाइड (m)	gaid
excursion, sightseeing tour	पर्यटन यात्रा (m)	paryatan yātra
to show (vt)	दिखाना	dikhāna

to tell (vt)	बताना	batāna
to find (vt)	ढूँढना	dhūnrhana
to get lost (lose one's way)	खो जाना	kho jāna
map (e.g. underground ~)	नक्शा (m)	naksha
map (e.g. city ~)	नक्शा (m)	naksha
souvenir, gift	यादगार (m)	yādagār
gift shop	गिफ़्ट शॉप (f)	gift shop
to take pictures	फोटो खींचना	foto khīnchana
to have one's picture taken	अपना फ़ोटो खिंचवाना	apana foto khinchavāna

TRANSPORT

23. Airport

airport	हवाई अड्डा (m)	havaī adda
aeroplane	विमान (m)	vimān
airline	हवाई कम्पनी (f)	havaī kampanī
air traffic controller	हवाई यातायात नियंत्रक (m)	havaī yātāyāt niyantrak
departure	प्रस्थान (m)	prasthān
arrival	आगमन (m)	āgaman
to arrive (by plane)	पहुंचना	pahunchana
departure time	उड़ान का समय (m)	urān ka samay
arrival time	आगमन का समय (m)	āgaman ka samay
to be delayed	देर से आना	der se āna
flight delay	उड़ान देरी (f)	urān derī
information board	सूचना बोर्ड (m)	sūchana bord
information	सूचना (f)	sūchana
to announce (vt)	घोषणा करना	ghoshana karana
flight (e.g. next ~)	फ्लाइट (f)	flait
customs	सीमाशुल्क कार्यालय (m)	sīmāshulk kāryālay
customs officer	सीमाशुल्क अधिकारी (m)	sīmāshulk adhikārī
customs declaration	सीमाशुल्क घोषणा (f)	sīmāshulk ghoshana
to fill in the declaration	सीमाशुल्क घोषणा भरना	sīmāshulk ghoshana bharana
passport control	पासपोर्ट जांच (f)	pāsport jānch
luggage	सामान (m)	sāmān
hand luggage	दस्ती सामान (m)	dastī sāmān
luggage trolley	सामान के लिये गाड़ी (f)	sāmān ke liye gārī
landing	विमानारोहण (m)	vimānārohan
landing strip	विमानारोहण मार्ग (m)	vimānārohan mārg
to land (vi)	उतरना	utarana
airstair (passenger stair)	सीढ़ी (f)	sīrhī
check-in	चेक-इन (m)	chek-in
check-in counter	चेक-इन डेस्क (m)	chek-in desk
to check-in (vi)	चेक-इन करना	chek-in karana
boarding card	बोर्डिंग पास (m)	bording pās
departure gate	प्रस्थान गेट (m)	prasthān get
transit	पारवहन (m)	pāravahan
to wait (vt)	इतज़ार करना	intazār karana
departure lounge	प्रतीक्षालय (m)	pratīkshālay
to see off	विदा करना	vida karana
to say goodbye	विदा कहना	vida kahana

24. Aeroplane

aeroplane	विमान (m)	vimān
air ticket	हवाई टिकट (m)	havaī tikat
airline	हवाई कम्पनी (f)	havaī kampanī
airport	हवाई अड्डा (m)	havaī adda
supersonic (adj)	पराध्वनिक	parādhvanik
captain	कप्तान (m)	kaptān
crew	वैमानिक दल (m)	vaimānik dal
pilot	विमान चालक (m)	vimān chālak
stewardess	एयर होस्टस (f)	eyar hostas
navigator	नैवीगेटर (m)	naivīgetar
wings	पंख (m pl)	pankh
tail	पूँछ (f)	pūnchh
cockpit	कॉकपिट (m)	kokapit
engine	इंजन (m)	injan
undercarriage (landing gear)	हवाई जहाज़ पहिये (m)	havaī jahāz pahiye
turbine	टरबाइन (f)	tarabain
propeller	प्रोपेलर (m)	propelar
black box	ब्लैक बॉक्स (m)	blaik boks
yoke (control column)	कंट्रोल कॉलम (m)	kantrol kolam
fuel	ईंधन (m)	īndhan
safety card	सुरक्षा-पत्र (m)	suraksha-patr
oxygen mask	ऑक्सीजन मास्क (m)	oksījan māsk
uniform	वर्दी (f)	vardī
lifejacket	बचाव पेटी (f)	bachāv petī
parachute	पैराशूट (m)	pairāshūt
takeoff	उड़ान (m)	urān
to take off (vi)	उड़ना	urana
runway	उड़ान पट्टी (f)	urān pattī
visibility	दृश्यता (f)	drshyata
flight (act of flying)	उड़ान (m)	urān
altitude	ऊंचाई (f)	ūnchaī
air pocket	वायु-पॉकेट (m)	vāyu-poket
seat	सीट (f)	sīt
headphones	हेडफ़ोन (m)	hedafon
folding tray (tray table)	ट्रे टेबल (f)	tre tebal
airplane window	हवाई जहाज़ की खिड़की (f)	havaī jahāz kī khirakī
aisle	गलियारा (m)	galiyāra

25. Train

train	रेलगाड़ी, ट्रेन (f)	relagārī, tren
commuter train	लोकल ट्रेन (f)	lokal tren
express train	तेज़ रेलगाड़ी (f)	tez relagārī
diesel locomotive	डीज़ल रेलगाड़ी (f)	dīzal relagārī

steam locomotive	स्टीम इंजन (f)	stīm injan
coach, carriage	कोच (f)	koch
buffet car	डाइनर (f)	dainar
rails	पटरियाँ (f)	patariyān
railway	रेलवे (f)	relave
sleeper (track support)	पटरियाँ (f)	patariyān
platform (railway ~)	प्लेटफॉर्म (m)	pletaform
platform (~ 1, 2, etc.)	प्लेटफॉर्म (m)	pletaform
semaphore	सिग्नल (m)	signal
station	स्टेशन (m)	steshan
train driver	इंजन ड्राइवर (m)	injan draivar
porter (of luggage)	कुली (m)	kulī
carriage attendant	कोच एटेंडेंट (m)	koch etendent
passenger	मुसाफ़िर (m)	musāfir
ticket inspector	टीटी (m)	tītī
corridor (in train)	गलियारा (m)	galiyāra
emergency brake	आपात ब्रेक (m)	āpāt brek
compartment	डिब्बा (m)	dibba
berth	बर्थ (f)	barth
upper berth	ऊपरी बर्थ (f)	ūparī barth
lower berth	निचली बर्थ (f)	nīchalī barth
bed linen, bedding	बिस्तर (m)	bistar
ticket	टिकट (m)	tikat
timetable	टाइम टेबुल (m)	taim taibul
information display	सूचना बोर्ड (m)	sūchana bord
to leave, to depart	चले जाना	chale jāna
departure (of a train)	रवानगी (f)	ravānagī
to arrive (ab. train)	पहुंचना	pahunchana
arrival	आगमन (m)	āgaman
to arrive by train	गाड़ी से पहुंचना	gārī se pahunchana
to get on the train	गाड़ी पकड़ना	gādī pakarana
to get off the train	गाड़ी से उतरना	gārī se utarana
train crash	दुर्घटनाग्रस्त (f)	durghatanāgrast
steam locomotive	स्टीम इंजन (m)	stīm injan
stoker, fireman	अग्निशामक (m)	agnishāmak
firebox	भट्ठी (f)	bhatthī
coal	कोयला (m)	koyala

26. Ship

ship	जहाज़ (m)	jahāz
vessel	जहाज़ (m)	jahāz
steamship	जहाज़ (m)	jahāz
riverboat	मोटर बोट (m)	motar bot

cruise ship	लाइनर (m)	lainar
cruiser	क्रूज़र (m)	krūzar
yacht	याख्ट (m)	yākht
tugboat	कर्षक पोत (m)	karshak pot
barge	बार्ज़ (f)	bārj
ferry	फेरी बोट (f)	ferī bot
sailing ship	पाल नाव (f)	pāl nāv
brigantine	बादबानी (f)	bādabānī
ice breaker	हिमभंजक पोत (m)	himabhanjak pot
submarine	पनडुब्बी (f)	panadubbī
boat (flat-bottomed ~)	नाव (m)	nāv
dinghy (lifeboat)	किश्ती (f)	kishtī
lifeboat	जीवन रक्षा किश्ती (f)	jīvan raksha kishtī
motorboat	मोटर बोट (m)	motar bot
captain	कसान (m)	kaptān
seaman	मल्लाह (m)	mallāh
sailor	मल्लाह (m)	mallāh
crew	वैमानिक दल (m)	vaimānik dal
boatswain	बोसुन (m)	bosun
ship's boy	बोसुन (m)	bosun
cook	रसोइया (m)	rasoiya
ship's doctor	पोत डाक्टर (m)	pot dāktar
deck	डेक (m)	dek
mast	मस्तूल (m)	mastūl
sail	पाल (m)	pāl
hold	कार्गी (m)	kārgo
bow (prow)	जहाज़ का अगड़ा हिस्सा (m)	jahāz ka agara hissa
stern	जहाज़ का पिछला हिस्सा (m)	jahāz ka pichhala hissa
oar	चप्पू (m)	chappū
screw propeller	जहाज़ की पंखी चलाने का पेंच (m)	jahāz kī pankhī chalāne ka pench
cabin	कैबिन (m)	kaibin
wardroom	मेस (f)	mes
engine room	मशीन-कमरा (m)	mashīn-kamara
bridge	ब्रिज (m)	brij
radio room	रेडियो केबिन (m)	rediyo kebin
wave (radio)	रेडियो तरंग (f)	rediyo tarang
logbook	जहाज़ी रजिस्टर (m)	jahāzī rajistar
spyglass	टेलिस्कोप (m)	teliskop
bell	घंटा (m)	ghanta
flag	झंडा (m)	jhanda
hawser (mooring ~)	रस्सा (m)	rassa
knot (bowline, etc.)	जहाज़ी गांठ (f)	jahāzī gānth
deckrails	रेलिंग (f)	reling
gangway	सीढ़ी (f)	sīrhī

anchor	लंगर (m)	langar
to weigh anchor	लंगर उठाना	langar uthāna
to drop anchor	लंगर डालना	langar dālana
anchor chain	लंगर की ज़जीर (f)	langar kī zajīr
port (harbour)	बंदरगाह (m)	bandaragāh
quay, wharf	घाट (m)	ghāt
to berth (moor)	किनारे लगना	kināre lagana
to cast off	रवाना होना	ravāna hona
trip, voyage	यात्रा (f)	yātra
cruise (sea trip)	जलयात्रा (f)	jalayātra
course (route)	दिशा (f)	disha
route (itinerary)	मार्ग (m)	mārg
fairway (safe water channel)	नाब्य जलपथ (m)	nāvy jalapath
shallows	छिछला पानी (m)	chhichhala pānī
to run aground	छिछले पानी में धसना	chhichhale pānī men dhansana
storm	तूफ़ान (m)	tufān
signal	सिग्नल (m)	signal
to sink (vi)	डूबना	dūbana
SOS (distress signal)	एसओएस	esoes
ring buoy	लाइफ़ ब्वाय (m)	laif bvāy

CITY

27. Urban transport

bus, coach	बस (f)	bas
tram	ट्रैम (m)	traim
trolleybus	ट्रॉलीबस (f)	trolības
route (bus ~)	मार्ग (m)	mārg
number (e.g. bus ~)	नम्बर (m)	nambar
to go by ...	के माध्यम से जाना	ke mādhyam se jāna
to get on (~ the bus)	सवार होना	savār hona
to get off ...	उतरना	utarana
stop (e.g. bus ~)	बस स्टॉप (m)	bas stop
next stop	अगला स्टॉप (m)	agala stop
terminus	अंतिम स्टेशन (m)	antim steshan
timetable	समय सारणी (f)	samay sāranī
to wait (vt)	इंतज़ार करना	intazār karana
ticket	टिकट (m)	tikat
fare	टिकट का किराया (m)	tikat ka kirāya
cashier (ticket seller)	कैशियर (m)	kaishiyar
ticket inspection	टिकट जाँच (f)	tikat jānch
ticket inspector	कंडक्टर (m)	kandaktar
to be late (for ...)	देर हो जाना	der ho jāna
to miss (~ the train, etc.)	छूट जाना	chhūt jāna
to be in a hurry	जल्दी में रहना	jaldī men rahana
taxi, cab	टैक्सी (m)	taiksī
taxi driver	टैक्सीवाला (m)	taiksīvāla
by taxi	टैक्सी से (m)	taiksī se
taxi rank	टैक्सी स्टैंड (m)	taiksī staind
to call a taxi	टैक्सी बुलाना	taiksī bulāna
to take a taxi	टैक्सी लेना	taiksī lena
traffic	यातायात (f)	yātāyāt
traffic jam	ट्रैफ़िक जाम (m)	traifik jām
rush hour	भीड़ का समय (m)	bhīr ka samay
to park (vi)	पार्क करना	pārk karana
to park (vt)	पार्क करना	pārk karana
car park	पार्किंग (f)	pārking
underground, tube	मेट्रो (m)	metro
station	स्टेशन (m)	steshan
to take the tube	मेट्रो लेना	metro lena
train	रेलगाड़ी, ट्रेन (f)	relagārī, tren
train station	स्टेशन (m)	steshan

28. City. Life in the city

city, town	नगर (m)	nagar
capital city	राजधानी (f)	rājadhānī
village	गांव (m)	gānv
city map	नगर का नक्शा (m)	nagar ka naksha
city centre	नगर का केन्द्र (m)	nagar ka kendr
suburb	उपनगर (m)	upanagar
suburban (adj)	उपनगरिक	upanagarik
outskirts	बाहरी इलाका (m)	bāharī ilāka
environs (suburbs)	इर्दगिर्द के इलाके (m pl)	irdagird ke ilāke
city block	सेक्टर (m)	sektar
residential block (area)	मुहल्ला (m)	muhalla
traffic	यातायात (f)	yātāyāt
traffic lights	यातायात सिग्नल (m)	yātāyāt signal
public transport	जन परिवहन (m)	jan parivahan
crossroads	चौराहा (m)	chaurāha
zebra crossing	ज़ेबरा क्रॉसिंग (f)	zebara krosing
pedestrian subway	पैदल यात्रियों के लिए अंडरपास (m)	paidal yātriyon ke lie andarapās
to cross (~ the street)	सड़क पार करना	sarak pār karana
pedestrian	पैदल-यात्री (m)	paidal-yātrī
pavement	फुटपाथ (m)	futapāth
bridge	पुल (m)	pul
embankment (river walk)	तट (m)	tat
fountain	फौवारा (m)	fauvāra
allée (garden walkway)	छायापथ (f)	chhāyāpath
park	पार्क (m)	pārk
boulevard	चौड़ी सड़क (m)	chaurī sarak
square	मैदान (m)	maidān
avenue (wide street)	मार्ग (m)	mārg
street	सड़क (f)	sarak
side street	गली (f)	galī
dead end	बंद गली (f)	band galī
house	मकान (m)	makān
building	इमारत (f)	imārat
skyscraper	गगनचुंबी भवन (f)	gaganachumbī bhavan
facade	अगवाड़ा (m)	agavāra
roof	छत (f)	chhat
window	खिड़की (f)	khirakī
arch	मेहराब (m)	meharāb
column	स्तंभ (m)	stambh
corner	कोना (m)	kona
shop window	दुकान का शो-केस (m)	dukān ka sho-kes
signboard (store sign, etc.)	साईनबोर्ड (m)	saīnabord
poster (e.g., playbill)	पोस्टर (m)	postar

advertising poster	विज्ञापन पोस्टर (m)	vigyāpan postar
hoarding	बिलबोर्ड (m)	bilabord
rubbish	कूड़ा (m)	kūra
rubbish bin	कूड़े का डिब्बा (m)	kūre ka dibba
to litter (vi)	कूड़ा-करकट डालना	kūra-karkat dālana
rubbish dump	डम्पिंग ग्राउंड (m)	damping graund
telephone box	फ़ोन बूथ (m)	fon būth
lamppost	बिजली का खंभा (m)	bijalī ka khambha
bench (park ~)	पार्क-बेंच (f)	pārk-bench
police officer	पुलिसवाला (m)	pulisavāla
police	पुलिस (m)	pulis
beggar	भिखारी (m)	bhikhārī
homeless (n)	बेघर (m)	beghar

29. Urban institutions

shop	दुकान (f)	dukān
chemist, pharmacy	दवाख़ाना (m)	davākhāna
optician (spectacles shop)	चश्मे की दुकान (f)	chashme kī dukān
shopping centre	शॉपिंग मॉल (m)	shoping mol
supermarket	सुपर बाज़ार (m)	supar bāzār
bakery	बेकरी (f)	bekarī
baker	बेकर (m)	bekar
cake shop	टॉफ़ी की दुकान (f)	tofī kī dukān
grocery shop	परचून की दुकान (f)	parachūn kī dukān
butcher shop	गोश्त की दुकान (f)	gosht kī dukān
greengrocer	सब्ज़ियों की दुकान (f)	sabziyon kī dukān
market	बाज़ार (m)	bāzār
coffee bar	कॉफ़ी हाउस (m)	kāfī haus
restaurant	रेस्टरॉं (m)	restarān
pub, bar	शराबख़ाना (m)	sharābakhāna
pizzeria	पिट्ज़ा की दुकान (f)	pitza kī dukān
hairdresser	नाई की दुकान (f)	naī kī dukān
post office	डाकघर (m)	dākaghar
dry cleaners	ड्राइक्लीनर (m)	draiklīnar
photo studio	फ़ोटो की दुकान (f)	foto kī dukān
shoe shop	जूते की दुकान (f)	jūte kī dukān
bookshop	किताबों की दुकान (f)	kitābon kī dukān
sports shop	खेलकूद की दुकान (f)	khelakūd kī dukān
clothes repair shop	कपड़ों की मरम्मत की दुकान (f)	kaparon kī marammat kī dukān
formal wear hire	कपड़ों को किराए पर देने की दुकान (f)	kaparon ko kirae par dene kī dukān
video rental shop	वीडियो रेन्टल दुकान (f)	vīdiyo rental dukān
circus	सर्कस (m)	sarkas

zoo	चिड़ियाघर (m)	chiriyāghar
cinema	सिनेमाघर (m)	sinemāghar
museum	संग्रहालय (m)	sangrahālay
library	पुस्तकालय (m)	pustakālay
theatre	रंगमंच (m)	rangamanch
opera (opera house)	ओपेरा (m)	opera
nightclub	नाईट क्लब (m)	naĩt klab
casino	केसिनो (m)	kesino
mosque	मस्जिद (m)	masjid
synagogue	सीनागोग (m)	sīnāgog
cathedral	गिरजाघर (m)	girajāghar
temple	मंदिर (m)	mandir
church	गिरजाघर (m)	girajāghar
college	कॉलेज (m)	kolej
university	विश्वविद्यालय (m)	vishvavidyālay
school	विद्यालय (m)	vidyālay
prefecture	प्रशासक प्रान्त (m)	prashāsak prānt
town hall	सिटी हॉल (m)	sitī hol
hotel	होटल (f)	hotal
bank	बैंक (m)	baink
embassy	दूतावस (m)	dūtāvas
travel agency	पर्यटन आफ़िस (m)	paryatan āfis
information office	पूछताछ कार्यालय (m)	pūchhatāchh kāryālay
currency exchange	मुद्रालय (m)	mudrālay
underground, tube	मेट्रो (m)	metro
hospital	अस्पताल (m)	aspatāl
petrol station	पेट्रोल पम्प (f)	petrol pamp
car park	पार्किंग (f)	pārking

30. Signs

signboard (store sign, etc.)	साईनबोर्ड (m)	saĩnabord
notice (door sign, etc.)	दुकान का साईन (m)	dukān ka saĩn
poster	पोस्टर (m)	postar
direction sign	दिशा संकेतक (m)	disha sanketak
arrow (sign)	तीर दिशा संकेतक (m)	tīr disha sanketak
caution	चेतावनी (f)	chetāvanī
warning sign	चेतावनी संकेतक (m)	chetāvanī sanketak
to warn (vt)	चेतावनी देना	chetāvanī dena
rest day (weekly ~)	छुट्टी का दिन (m)	chhuttī ka din
timetable (schedule)	समय सारणी (f)	samay sāranī
opening hours	खुलने का समय (m)	khulane ka samay
WELCOME!	आपका स्वागत है!	āpaka svāgat hai!
ENTRANCE	प्रवेश	pravesh

WAY OUT	निकास	nikās
PUSH	धक्का दें	dhakka den
PULL	खींचे	khīnche
OPEN	खुला	khula
CLOSED	बंद	band

| WOMEN | औरतों के लिये | auraton ke liye |
| MEN | आदमियों के लिये | ādamiyon ke liye |

DISCOUNTS	डिस्काउन्ट	diskaunt
SALE	सेल	sel
NEW!	नया!	naya!
FREE	मुफ्त	muft

ATTENTION!	ध्यान दें!	dhyān den!
NO VACANCIES	कोई जगह खाली नहीं है	koī jagah khālī nahin hai
RESERVED	रिज़र्वेड	rizarvad

| ADMINISTRATION | प्रशासन | prashāsan |
| STAFF ONLY | केवल कर्मचारियों के लिए | keval karmachāriyon ke lie |

BEWARE OF THE DOG!	कुत्ते से सावधान!	kutte se sāvadhān!
NO SMOKING	धूम्रपान निषेध!	dhumrapān nishedh!
DO NOT TOUCH!	छूना मना!	chhūna mana!

DANGEROUS	खतरा	khatara
DANGER	खतरा	khatara
HIGH VOLTAGE	उच्च वोल्टेज	uchch voltej
NO SWIMMING!	तैरना मना!	tairana mana!
OUT OF ORDER	ख़राब	kharāb

FLAMMABLE	ज्वलनशील	jvalanashīl
FORBIDDEN	निषिद्ध	nishiddh
NO TRESPASSING!	प्रवेश निषेध!	pravesh nishedh!
WET PAINT	गीला पेंट	gīla pent

31. Shopping

to buy (purchase)	खरीदना	kharīdana
shopping	खरीदारी (f)	kharīdārī
to go shopping	खरीदारी करने जाना	kharīdārī karane jāna
shopping	खरीदारी (f)	kharīdārī

| to be open (ab. shop) | खुला होना | khula hona |
| to be closed | बन्द होना | band hona |

footwear, shoes	जूता (m)	jūta
clothes, clothing	पोशाक (m)	poshāk
cosmetics	शृंगार-सामग्री (f)	shrrngār-sāmagrī
food products	खाने-पीने की चीज़ें (f pl)	khāne-pīne kī chīzen
gift, present	उपहार (m)	upahār

| shop assistant (masc.) | बेचनेवाला (m) | bechanevāla |
| shop assistant (fem.) | बेचनेवाली (f) | bechanevālī |

cash desk	कैश-काउन्टर (m)	kaish-kauntar
mirror	आईना (m)	āīna
counter (shop ~)	काउन्टर (m)	kauntar
fitting room	ट्राई करने का कमरा (m)	traī karane ka kamara

to try on	ट्राई करना	traī karana
to fit (ab. dress, etc.)	फिटिंग करना	fiting karana
to fancy (vt)	पसंद करना	pasand karana

price	दाम (m)	dām
price tag	प्राइस टैग (m)	prais taig
to cost (vt)	दाम होना	dām hona
How much?	कितना?	kitana?
discount	डिस्काउन्ट (m)	diskaunt

inexpensive (adj)	सस्ता	sasta
cheap (adj)	सस्ता	sasta
expensive (adj)	महंगा	mahanga
It's expensive	यह महंगा है	yah mahanga hai

hire (n)	रेन्टल (m)	rental
to hire (~ a dinner jacket)	किराए पर लेना	kirae par lena
credit (trade credit)	क्रेडिट (m)	kredit
on credit (adv)	क्रेडिट पर	kredit par

CLOTHING & ACCESSORIES

32. Outerwear. Coats

clothes	कपड़े (m)	kapare
outerwear	बाहरी पोशाक (m)	bāharī poshāk
winter clothing	सर्दियों की पोशाक (f)	sardiyon kī poshak
coat (overcoat)	ओवरकोट (m)	ovarakot
fur coat	फरकोट (m)	farakot
fur jacket	फ़र की जैकेट (f)	far kī jaiket
down coat	फ़ेदर कोट (m)	fedar kot
jacket (e.g. leather ~)	जैकेट (f)	jaiket
raincoat (trenchcoat, etc.)	बरसाती (f)	barasātī
waterproof (adj)	जलरोधक	jalarodhak

33. Men's & women's clothing

shirt (button shirt)	कमीज़ (f)	kamīz
trousers	पैंट (m)	paint
jeans	जीन्स (m)	jīns
suit jacket	कोट (m)	kot
suit	सूट (m)	sūt
dress (frock)	फ्रॉक (f)	frok
skirt	स्कर्ट (f)	skart
blouse	ब्लाउज़ (f)	blauz
knitted jacket (cardigan, etc.)	कार्डिगन (f)	kārdigan
jacket (of a woman's suit)	जैकेट (f)	jaiket
T-shirt	टी-शर्ट (f)	tī-shart
shorts (short trousers)	शोर्ट्स (m pl)	shorts
tracksuit	ट्रैक सूट (m)	traik sūt
bathrobe	बाथ रोब (m)	bāth rob
pyjamas	पजामा (m)	pajāma
jumper (sweater)	सूटर (m)	sūtar
pullover	पुलोवर (m)	pulovar
waistcoat	बण्डी (m)	bandī
tailcoat	टेल-कोट (m)	tel-kot
dinner suit	डिनर-जैकेट (f)	dinar-jaiket
uniform	वर्दी (f)	vardī
workwear	वर्दी (f)	vardī
boiler suit	ओवरऑल्स (m)	ovarols
coat (e.g. doctor's smock)	कोट (m)	kot

34. Clothing. Underwear

underwear	अंगवस्त्र (m)	angavastr
vest (singlet)	बनियान (f)	baniyān
socks	मोज़े (m pl)	moze
nightdress	नाइट गाउन (m)	nait gaun
bra	ब्रा (f)	bra
knee highs (knee-high socks)	घुटनों तक के मोज़े (m)	ghutanon tak ke moze
tights	टाइट्स (m pl)	taits
stockings (hold ups)	स्टाकिंग (m pl)	stāking
swimsuit, bikini	स्विम सूट (m)	svim sūt

35. Headwear

hat	टोपी (f)	topī
trilby hat	हैट (f)	hait
baseball cap	बैस्बॉल कैप (f)	baisbol kaip
flatcap	फ्लैट कैप (f)	flait kaip
beret	बेरेट (m)	beret
hood	हूड (m)	hūd
panama hat	पनामा हैट (m)	panāma hait
knit cap (knitted hat)	बुनी हुई टोपी (f)	bunī huī topī
headscarf	सिर का स्कार्फ़ (m)	sir ka skārf
women's hat	महिलाओं की टोपी (f)	mahilaon kī topī
hard hat	हेलमेट (f)	helamet
forage cap	पुलिसीया टोपी (f)	pulisīya topī
helmet	हेलमेट (f)	helamet
bowler	बॉलर हैट (m)	bolar hait
top hat	टॉप हैट (m)	top hait

36. Footwear

footwear	पनही (f)	panahī
shoes (men's shoes)	जूते (m pl)	jūte
shoes (women's shoes)	जूते (m pl)	jūte
boots (e.g., cowboy ~)	बूट (m pl)	būt
carpet slippers	चप्पल (f pl)	chappal
trainers	टेनिस के जूते (m)	tenis ke jūte
trainers	स्नीकर्स (m)	snīkars
sandals	सैन्डल (f)	saindal
cobbler (shoe repairer)	मोची (m)	mochī
heel	एडी (f)	erī
pair (of shoes)	जोड़ा (m)	jora
lace (shoelace)	जूते का फ़ीता (m)	jūte ka fīta

to lace up (vt)	फ़ीता बाँधना	fīta bāndhana
shoehorn	शू-होर्न (m)	shū-horn
shoe polish	बूट-पालिश (m)	būt-pālish

37. Personal accessories

gloves	दस्ताने (m pl)	dastāne
mittens	दस्ताने (m pl)	dastāne
scarf (muffler)	मफ़लर (m)	mafalar

glasses	ऐनक (m pl)	ainak
frame (eyeglass ~)	चश्मे का फ्रेम (m)	chashme ka frem
umbrella	छतरी (f)	chhatarī
walking stick	छड़ी (f)	chharī
hairbrush	ब्रश (m)	brash
fan	पंखा (m)	pankha

tie (necktie)	टाई (f)	taī
bow tie	बो टाई (f)	bo taī
braces	पतलून बाँधने का फ़ीता (m)	patalūn bāndhane ka fīta
handkerchief	रूमाल (m)	rūmāl

comb	कंघा (m)	kangha
hair slide	बालपिन (f)	bālapin
hairpin	हेयरक्लीप (f)	heyaraklīp
buckle	बकसुआ (m)	bakasua

| belt | बेल्ट (m) | belt |
| shoulder strap | कंधे का पट्टा (m) | kandhe ka patta |

bag (handbag)	बैग (m)	baig
handbag	पर्स (m)	pars
rucksack	बैकपैक (m)	baikapaik

38. Clothing. Miscellaneous

fashion	फ़ैशन (m)	faishan
in vogue (adj)	प्रचलन में	prachalan men
fashion designer	फ़ैशन डिज़ाइनर (m)	faishan dizainar

collar	कॉलर (m)	kolar
pocket	जेब (m)	jeb
pocket (as adj)	जेब	jeb
sleeve	आस्तीन (f)	āstīn
hanging loop	हैंगिंग लूप (f)	hainging lūp
flies (on trousers)	ज़िप (f)	zip

zip (fastener)	ज़िप (f)	zip
fastener	हुक (m)	huk
button	बटन (m)	batan
buttonhole	बटन का काज (m)	batan ka kāj
to come off (ab. button)	निकल जाना	nikal jāna

to sew (vi, vt)	सीना	sīna
to embroider (vi, vt)	काढ़ना	kārhana
embroidery	कढ़ाई (f)	karhaī
sewing needle	सूई (f)	sūī
thread	धागा (m)	dhāga
seam	सीवन (m)	sīvan
to get dirty (vi)	मैला होना	maila hona
stain (mark, spot)	धब्बा (m)	dhabba
to crease, to crumple	शिकन पड़ जाना	shikan par jāna
to tear, to rip (vt)	फट जाना	fat jāna
clothes moth	कपड़ों के कीड़े (m)	kaparon ke kīre

39. Personal care. Cosmetics

toothpaste	टूथपेस्ट (m)	tūthapest
toothbrush	टूथब्रश (m)	tūthabrash
to clean one's teeth	दाँत साफ़ करना	dānt sāf karana
razor	रेज़र (f)	rezar
shaving cream	हजामत का क्रीम (m)	hajāmat ka krīm
to shave (vi)	शेव करना	shev karana
soap	साबुन (m)	sābun
shampoo	शैम्पू (m)	shaimpū
scissors	कैंची (f pl)	kainchī
nail file	नाख़ून चिसनी (f)	nākhūn ghisanī
nail clippers	नाख़ून कतरनी (f)	nākhūn kataranī
tweezers	ट्वीज़र्स (f)	tvīzars
cosmetics	श्रृंगार-सामग्री (f)	shrrngār-sāmagrī
face mask	चेहरे का लेप (m)	chehare ka lep
manicure	मैनीक्योर (m)	mainīkyor
to have a manicure	मैनीक्योर करवाना	mainīkyor karavāna
pedicure	पेडिक्यूर (m)	pedikyūr
make-up bag	श्रृंगार थैली (f)	shrrngār thailī
face powder	पाउडर (m)	paudar
powder compact	कॉम्पैक्ट पाउडर (m)	kompaikt paudar
blusher	ब्लशर (m)	blashar
perfume (bottled)	ख़ुशबू (f)	khushabū
toilet water (lotion)	टॉयलेट वॉटर (m)	tāyalet votar
lotion	लोशन (m)	loshan
cologne	कोलोन (m)	kolon
eyeshadow	आई-शैडो (m)	āī-shaido
eyeliner	आई-पेंसिल (f)	āī-pensil
mascara	मस्कारा (m)	maskāra
lipstick	लिपस्टिक (m)	lipastik
nail polish	नेल पॉलिश (f)	nel polish
hair spray	हेयर स्प्रे (m)	heyar spre

deodorant	डिओडरेन्ट (m)	diodarent
cream	क्रीम (m)	krīm
face cream	चेहरे की क्रीम (f)	chehare kī krīm
hand cream	हाथ की क्रीम (f)	hāth kī krīm
anti-wrinkle cream	एंटी रिंकल क्रीम (f)	entī rinkal krīm
day (as adj)	दिन का	din ka
night (as adj)	रात का	rāt ka
tampon	टैम्पन (m)	taimpan
toilet paper (toilet roll)	टॉयलेट पेपर (m)	toyalet pepar
hair dryer	हेयर ड्रायर (m)	heyar drāyar

40. Watches. Clocks

watch (wristwatch)	घड़ी (f pl)	gharī
dial	डायल (m)	dāyal
hand (clock, watch)	सुई (f)	suī
metal bracelet	धातु से बनी घड़ी का पट्टा (m)	dhātu se banī gharī ka patta
watch strap	घड़ी का पट्टा (m)	gharī ka patta
battery	बैटरी (f)	baiterī
to be flat (battery)	ख़त्म हो जाना	khatm ho jāna
to change a battery	बैटरी बदलना	baiterī badalana
to run fast	तेज़ चलना	tez chalana
to run slow	धीमी चलना	dhīmī chalana
wall clock	दीवार-घड़ी (f pl)	dīvār-gharī
hourglass	रेत-घड़ी (f pl)	ret-gharī
sundial	सूरज-घड़ी (f pl)	sūraj-gharī
alarm clock	अलार्म घड़ी (f)	alārm gharī
watchmaker	घड़ीसाज़ (m)	gharīsāz
to repair (vt)	मरम्मत करना	marammat karana

EVERYDAY EXPERIENCE

41. Money

money	पैसा (m pl)	paisa
currency exchange	मुद्रा विनिमय (m)	mudra vinimay
exchange rate	विनिमय दर (m)	vinimay dar
cashpoint	एटीएम (m)	etīem
coin	सिक्का (m)	sikka
dollar	डॉलर (m)	dolar
euro	यूरो (m)	yūro
lira	लीरा (f)	līra
Deutschmark	डचमार्क (m)	dachamārk
franc	फ्रांक (m)	frānk
pound sterling	पाउन्ड स्टरलिंग (m)	paund staraling
yen	येन (m)	yen
debt	कर्ज़ (m)	karz
debtor	कर्ज़दार (m)	qarzadār
to lend (money)	कर्ज़ देना	karz dena
to borrow (vi, vt)	कर्ज़ लेना	karz lena
bank	बैंक (m)	baink
account	बैंक खाता (m)	baink khāta
to deposit into the account	बैंक खाते में जमा करना	baink khāte men jama karana
to withdraw (vt)	खाते से पैसे निकालना	khāte se paise nikālana
credit card	क्रेडिट कार्ड (m)	kredit kārd
cash	कैश (m pl)	kaish
cheque	चेक (m)	chek
to write a cheque	चेक लिखना	chek likhana
chequebook	चेकबुक (f)	chekabuk
wallet	बटुआ (m)	batua
purse	बटुआ (m)	batua
safe	लॉकर (m)	lokar
heir	उत्तराधिकारी (m)	uttarādhikārī
inheritance	उत्तराधिकार (m)	uttarādhikār
fortune (wealth)	संपत्ति (f)	sampatti
lease	किराये पर देना (m)	kirāye par dena
rent (money)	किराया (m)	kirāya
to rent (sth from sb)	किराए पर लेना	kirae par lena
price	दाम (m)	dām
cost	कीमत (f)	kīmat
sum	रक़म (m)	raqam

to spend (vt)	खर्च करना	kharch karana
expenses	खर्च (m pl)	kharch
to economize (vi, vt)	बचत करना	bachat karana
economical	किफ़ायती	kifāyatī
to pay (vi, vt)	दाम चुकाना	dām chukāna
payment	भुगतान (m)	bhugatān
change (give the ~)	चिल्लर (m)	chillar
tax	टैक्स (m)	taiks
fine	जुर्माना (m)	jurmāna
to fine (vt)	जुर्माना लगाना	jurmāna lagāna

42. Post. Postal service

post office	डाकघर (m)	dākaghar
post (letters, etc.)	डाक (m)	dāk
postman	डाकिया (m)	dākiya
opening hours	खुलने का समय (m)	khulane ka samay
letter	पत्र (m)	patr
registered letter	रजिस्टरी पत्र (m)	rajistarī patr
postcard	पोस्ट कार्ड (m)	post kārd
telegram	तार (m)	tār
parcel	पार्सल (f)	pārsal
money transfer	मनी ट्रांसफर (m)	manī trānsafar
to receive (vt)	पाना	pāna
to send (vt)	भेजना	bhejana
sending	भेज (m)	bhej
address	पता (m)	pata
postcode	पिन कोड (m)	pin kod
sender	भेजनेवाला (m)	bhejanevāla
receiver	पानेवाला (m)	pānevāla
name (first name)	पहला नाम (m)	pahala nām
surname (last name)	उपनाम (m)	upanām
postage rate	डाक दर (m)	dāk dar
standard (adj)	मानक	mānak
economical (adj)	किफ़ायती	kifāyatī
weight	वज़न (m)	vazan
to weigh (~ letters)	तोलना	tolana
envelope	लिफ़ाफ़ा (m)	lifāfa
postage stamp	डाक टिकट (m)	dāk tikat
to stamp an envelope	डाक टिकट लगाना	dāk tikat lagāna

43. Banking

bank	बैंक (m)	baink
branch (of a bank)	शाखा (f)	shākha

| consultant | क्लर्क (m) | klark |
| manager (director) | मैनेजर (m) | mainejar |

bank account	बैंक खाता (m)	baink khāta
account number	खाते का नम्बर (m)	khāte ka nambar
current account	चालू खाता (m)	chālū khāta
deposit account	बचत खाता (m)	bachat khāta

to open an account	खाता खोलना	khāta kholana
to close the account	खाता बंद करना	khāta band karana
to deposit into the account	खाते में जमा करना	khāte men jama karana
to withdraw (vt)	खाते से पैसा निकालना	khāte se paisa nikālana

deposit	जमा (m)	jama
to make a deposit	जमा करना	jama karana
wire transfer	तार स्थानांतरण (m)	tār sthānāntaran
to wire, to transfer	पैसे स्थानांतरित करना	paise sthānāntarit karana

| sum | रक़म (m) | raqam |
| How much? | कितना? | kitana? |

| signature | हस्ताक्षर (f) | hastākshar |
| to sign (vt) | हस्ताक्षर करना | hastākshar karana |

credit card	क्रेडिट कार्ड (m)	kredit kārd
code (PIN code)	पिन कोड (m)	pin kod
credit card number	क्रेडिट कार्ड संख्या (f)	kredit kārd sankhya
cashpoint	एटीएम (m)	etīem

cheque	चेक (m)	chek
to write a cheque	चेक लिखना	chek likhana
chequebook	चेकबुक (f)	chekabuk

loan (bank ~)	उधार (m)	uthār
to apply for a loan	उधार के लिए आवेदन करना	udhār ke lie āvedan karana
to get a loan	उधार लेना	uthār lena
to give a loan	उधार देना	uthār dena
guarantee	गारन्टी (f)	gārantī

44. Telephone. Phone conversation

telephone	फ़ोन (m)	fon
mobile phone	मोबाइल फ़ोन (m)	mobail fon
answerphone	जवाबी मशीन (f)	javābī mashīn

| to call (by phone) | फ़ोन करना | fon karana |
| call, ring | कॉल (m) | kol |

to dial a number	नम्बर लगाना	nambar lagāna
Hello!	हेलो!	helo!
to ask (vt)	पूछना	pūchhana
to answer (vi, vt)	जवाब देना	javāb dena
to hear (vt)	सुनना	sunana
well (adv)	ठीक	thīk

not well (adv)	ठीक नहीं	thīk nahin
noises (interference)	आवाज़ें (f)	āvāzen
receiver	रिसीवर (m)	risīvar
to pick up (~ the phone)	फ़ोन उठाना	fon uthāna
to hang up (~ the phone)	फ़ोन रखना	fon rakhana
busy (engaged)	बिज़ी	bizī
to ring (ab. phone)	फ़ोन बजना	fon bajana
telephone book	टेलीफ़ोन बुक (m)	telīfon buk
local (adj)	लोकल	lokal
trunk (e.g. ~ call)	लंबी दूरी की कॉल	lambī dūrī kī kol
international (adj)	अंतर्राष्ट्रीय	antarrāshtrīy

45. Mobile telephone

mobile phone	मोबाइल फ़ोन (m)	mobail fon
display	डिस्प्ले (m)	disple
button	बटन (m)	batan
SIM card	सिम कार्ड (m)	sim kārd
battery	बैटरी (f)	baitarī
to be flat (battery)	बैटरी डेड हो जाना	baitarī ded ho jāna
charger	चार्जर (m)	chārjar
menu	मीनू (m)	mīnū
settings	सेटिंग्स (f)	setings
tune (melody)	कॉलर ट्यून (m)	kolar tyūn
to select (vt)	चुनना	chunana
calculator	कैल्कुलैटर (m)	kailkulaitar
voice mail	वॉयस मेल (f)	voyas mel
alarm clock	अलार्म घड़ी (f)	alārm gharī
contacts	संपर्क (m)	sampark
SMS (text message)	एसएमएस (m)	esemes
subscriber	सदस्य (m)	sadasy

46. Stationery

ballpoint pen	बॉल पेन (m)	bol pen
fountain pen	फाउन्टेन पेन (m)	faunten pen
pencil	पेंसिल (f)	pensil
highlighter	हाइलाइटर (m)	hailaitar
felt-tip pen	फ़ेल्ट टिप पेन (m)	felt tip pen
notepad	नोटबुक (m)	notabuk
diary	डायरी (f)	dāyarī
ruler	स्केल (m)	skel
calculator	कैल्कुलेटर (m)	kailkuletar

rubber	रबड़ (f)	rabar
drawing pin	थंबटैक (m)	thanrbataik
paper clip	पेपर क्लिप (m)	pepar klip

glue	गोंद (f)	gond
stapler	स्टेप्लर (m)	steplar
hole punch	होल पंचर (m)	hol panchar
pencil sharpener	शार्पनर (m)	shārpanar

47. Foreign languages

language	भाषा (f)	bhāsha
foreign language	विदेशी भाषा (f)	videshī bhāsha
to study (vt)	पढ़ना	parhana
to learn (language, etc.)	सीखना	sīkhana

to read (vi, vt)	पढ़ना	parhana
to speak (vi, vt)	बोलना	bolana
to understand (vt)	समझना	samajhana
to write (vt)	लिखना	likhana

fast (adv)	तेज़	tez
slowly (adv)	धीरे	dhīre
fluently (adv)	धड़ल्ले से	dharalle se

rules	नियम (m pl)	niyam
grammar	व्याकरण (m)	vyākaran
vocabulary	शब्दावली (f)	shabdāvalī
phonetics	स्वरविज्ञान (m)	svaravigyān

textbook	पाठ्यपुस्तक (f)	pāṭhyapustak
dictionary	शब्दकोश (m)	shabdakosh
teach-yourself book	स्वयंशिक्षक पुस्तक (m)	svayanshikshak pustak
phrasebook	वार्तालाप-पुस्तिका (f)	vārttālāp-pustika

cassette, tape	कैसेट (f)	kaiset
videotape	वीडियो कैसेट (m)	vīdiyo kaiset
CD, compact disc	सीडी (m)	sīdī
DVD	डीवीडी (m)	dīvīdī

alphabet	वर्णमाला (f)	varnamāla
to spell (vt)	हिज्जे करना	hijje karana
pronunciation	उच्चारण (m)	uchchāran

accent	लहज़ा (m)	lahaza
with an accent	लहज़े के साथ	lahaze ke sāth
without an accent	बिना लहज़े	bina lahaze

| word | शब्द (m) | shabd |
| meaning | मतलब (m) | matalab |

course (e.g. a French ~)	पाठ्यक्रम (m)	pāṭhyakram
to sign up	सदस्य बनना	sadasy banana
teacher	शिक्षक (m)	shikshak

translation (process)	तर्जुमा (m)	tarjuma
translation (text, etc.)	अनुवाद (m)	anuvād
translator	अनुवादक (m)	anuvādak
interpreter	दुभाषिया (m)	dubhāshiya
polyglot	बहुभाषी (m)	bahubhāshī
memory	स्मृति (f)	smrti

MEALS. RESTAURANT

48. Table setting

spoon	चम्मच (m)	chammach
knife	छुरी (f)	chhurī
fork	काँटा (m)	kānta
cup (e.g., coffee ~)	प्याला (m)	pyāla
plate (dinner ~)	तश्तरी (f)	tashtarī
saucer	साँसर (m)	sosar
serviette	नैपकीन (m)	naipakīn
toothpick	टूथपिक (m)	tūthapik

49. Restaurant

restaurant	रेस्टराँ (m)	restarān
coffee bar	कॉफ़ी हाउस (m)	kofī haus
pub, bar	बार (m)	bār
tearoom	चायख़ाना (m)	chāyakhāna
waiter	बैरा (m)	baira
waitress	बैरी (f)	bairī
barman	बारमैन (m)	bāramain
menu	मेनू (m)	menū
wine list	वाइन सूची (f)	vain sūchī
to book a table	मेज़ बुक करना	mez buk karana
course, dish	पकवान (m)	pakavān
to order (meal)	आर्डर देना	ārdar dena
to make an order	आर्डर देना	ārdar dena
aperitif	एपेरेतीफ़ (m)	eperetīf
starter	एपेटाइज़र (m)	epetaizar
dessert, pudding	मीठा (m)	mītha
bill	बिल (m)	bil
to pay the bill	बील का भुगतान करना	bīl ka bhugatān karana
to give change	खुले पैसे देना	khule paise dena
tip	टिप (f)	tip

50. Meals

food	खाना (m)	khāna
to eat (vi, vt)	खाना खाना	khāna khāna

breakfast	नाश्ता (m)	nāshta
to have breakfast	नाश्ता करना	nāshta karana
lunch	दोपहर का भोजन (m)	dopahar ka bhojan
to have lunch	दोपहर का भोजन करना	dopahar ka bhojan karana
dinner	रात्रिभोज (m)	rātribhoj
to have dinner	रात्रिभोज करना	rātribhoj karana

| appetite | भूख (f) | bhūkh |
| Enjoy your meal! | अपने भोजन का आनंद उठाएं! | apane bhojan ka ānand uthaen! |

to open (~ a bottle)	खोलना	kholana
to spill (liquid)	गिराना	girāna
to spill out (vi)	गिराना	girāna

to boil (vi)	उबालना	ubālana
to boil (vt)	उबालना	ubālana
boiled (~ water)	उबला हुआ	ubala hua
to chill, cool down (vt)	ठंडा करना	thanda karana
to chill (vi)	ठंडा करना	thanda karana

| taste, flavour | स्वाद (m) | svād |
| aftertaste | स्वाद (m) | svād |

to slim down (lose weight)	वज़न घटाना	vazan ghatāna
diet	डाइट (m)	dait
vitamin	विटामिन (m)	vitāmin
calorie	कैलोरी (f)	kailorī
vegetarian (n)	शाकाहारी (m)	shākāhārī
vegetarian (adj)	शाकाहारी	shākāhārī

fats (nutrient)	वसा (m pl)	vasa
proteins	प्रोटीन (m pl)	protīn
carbohydrates	कार्बोहाइड्रेट (m)	kārbohaidret
slice (of lemon, ham)	टुकड़ा (m)	tukara
piece (of cake, pie)	टुकड़ा (m)	tukara
crumb (of bread, cake, etc.)	टुकड़ा (m)	tukara

51. Cooked dishes

course, dish	पकवान (m)	pakavān
cuisine	व्यंजन (m)	vyanjan
recipe	रैसीपी (f)	raisīpī
portion	भाग (m)	bhāg

| salad | सलाद (m) | salād |
| soup | सूप (m) | sūp |

clear soup (broth)	यख़नी (f)	yakhanī
sandwich (bread)	सैन्डविच (m)	saindavich
fried eggs	आमलेट (m)	āmalet

| hamburger (beefburger) | हैमबर्गर (m) | haimabargar |
| beefsteak | बीफ़स्टीक (m) | bīfastīk |

side dish	साइड डिश (f)	said dish
spaghetti	स्पेघेटी (f)	speghetī
mash	आलू भरता (f)	ālū bharata
pizza	पीट्ज़ा (f)	pītza
porridge (oatmeal, etc.)	दलिया (f)	daliya
omelette	आमलेट (m)	āmalet
boiled (e.g. ~ beef)	उबला	ubala
smoked (adj)	धुएँ में पकाया हुआ	dhuen men pakāya hua
fried (adj)	भुना	bhuna
dried (adj)	सूखा	sūkha
frozen (adj)	फ्रोज़न	frozan
pickled (adj)	अचार	achār
sweet (sugary)	मीठा	mīṭha
salty (adj)	नमकीन	namakīn
cold (adj)	ठंडा	thanda
hot (adj)	गरम	garam
bitter (adj)	कड़वा	karava
tasty (adj)	स्वादिष्ट	svādisht
to cook in boiling water	उबलते पानी में पकाना	ubalate pānī men pakāna
to cook (dinner)	खाना बनाना	khāna banāna
to fry (vt)	भूनना	bhūnana
to heat up (food)	गरम करना	garam karana
to salt (vt)	नमक डालना	namak dālana
to pepper (vt)	मिर्च डालना	mirch dālana
to grate (vt)	कद्दूकश करना	kaddūkash karana
peel (n)	छिलका (f)	chhilaka
to peel (vt)	छिलका निकलना	chhilaka nikalana

52. Food

meat	गोश्त (m)	gosht
chicken	चीकन (m)	chīkan
poussin	रॉक कोर्निश मुर्गी (f)	rok kornish murgī
duck	बतख़ (f)	battakh
goose	हंस (m)	hans
game	शिकार के पशुपक्षी (f)	shikār ke pashupakshī
turkey	टर्की (m)	tarkī
pork	सुअर का गोश्त (m)	suar ka gosht
veal	बछड़े का गोश्त (m)	bachhare ka gosht
lamb	भेड़ का गोश्त (m)	bher ka gosht
beef	गाय का गोश्त (m)	gāy ka gosht
rabbit	खरगोश (m)	kharagosh
sausage (bologna, etc.)	सॉसेज (f)	sosej
vienna sausage (frankfurter)	वियना सॉसेज (m)	viyana sosej
bacon	बेकन (m)	bekan
ham	हैम (m)	haim
gammon	सुअर की जांघ (f)	suar kī jāngh
pâté	पिसा हुआ गोश्त (m)	pisa hua gosht

liver	जिगर (f)	jigar
mince (minced meat)	कीमा (m)	kīma
tongue	जीभ (m)	jībh

egg	अंडा (m)	anda
eggs	अंडे (m pl)	ande
egg white	अंडे की सफ़ेदी (m)	ande kī safedī
egg yolk	अंडे की ज़र्दी (m)	ande kī zardī

fish	मछली (f)	machhalī
seafood	समुद्री खाना (m)	samudrī khāna
caviar	मछली के अंडे (m)	machhalī ke ande

crab	केकड़ा (m)	kekara
prawn	चिंगड़ा (m)	chingara
oyster	सीप (m)	sīp
spiny lobster	लोबस्टर (m)	lobastar
octopus	ओक्टोपस (m)	oktopas
squid	स्कीड (m)	skīd

sturgeon	स्टर्जन (f)	starjan
salmon	सालमन (m)	sālaman
halibut	हैलिबट (f)	hailibat

cod	कॉड (f)	kod
mackerel	माक्रैल (f)	mākrail
tuna	टूना (f)	tūna
eel	बाम मछली (f)	bām machhalī

trout	ट्राउट मछली (f)	traut machhalī
sardine	सार्डीन (f)	sārdīn
pike	पाइक (f)	paik
herring	हेरिंग मछली (f)	hering machhalī

bread	ब्रेड (f)	bred
cheese	पनीर (m)	panīr
sugar	चीनी (f)	chīnī
salt	नमक (m)	namak

rice	चावल (m)	chāval
pasta (macaroni)	पास्ता (m)	pāsta
noodles	नूडल्स (m)	nūdals

butter	मक्खन (m)	makkhan
vegetable oil	तेल (m)	tel
sunflower oil	सूरजमुखी तेल (m)	sūrajamukhī tel
margarine	नकली मक्खन (m)	nakalī makkhan

| olives | जैतून (m) | jaitūn |
| olive oil | जैतून का तेल (m) | jaitūn ka tel |

milk	दूध (m)	dūdh
condensed milk	रबड़ी (f)	rabarī
yogurt	दही (m)	dahī
soured cream	खट्टी क्रीम (f)	khattī krīm
cream (of milk)	मलाई (f pl)	malāī

| mayonnaise | मेयोनेज़ (m) | meyonez |
| buttercream | क्रीम (m) | krīm |

groats (barley ~, etc.)	अनाज के दाने (m)	anāj ke dāne
flour	आटा (m)	āta
tinned food	डिब्बाबन्द खाना (m)	dibbāband khāna

cornflakes	कॉर्नफ़्लेक्स (m)	kornafleks
honey	शहद (m)	shahad
jam	जैम (m)	jaim
chewing gum	चूइन्ग गम (m)	chūing gam

53. Drinks

water	पानी (m)	pānī
drinking water	पीने का पानी (f)	pīne ka pānī
mineral water	मिनरल वॉटर (m)	minaral votar

still (adj)	स्टिल वॉटर	stil votar
carbonated (adj)	कार्बोनेटेड	kārboneted
sparkling (adj)	स्पार्कलिंग	spārkaling
ice	बर्फ़ (m)	barf
with ice	बर्फ़ के साथ	barf ke sāth

non-alcoholic (adj)	शराब रहित	sharāb rahit
soft drink	कोल्ड ड्रिंक (f)	kold drink
refreshing drink	शीतलक ड्रिंक (f)	shītalak drink
lemonade	लेमोनेड (m)	lemoned

spirits	शराब (m pl)	sharāb
wine	वाइन (f)	vain
white wine	सफ़ेद वाइन (f)	safed vain
red wine	लाल वाइन (f)	lāl vain

liqueur	लिकर (m)	likar
champagne	शैम्पेन (f)	shaimpen
vermouth	वर्माउथ (f)	varmauth

whisky	विस्की (f)	viskī
vodka	वोडका (m)	vodaka
gin	जिन (f)	jin
cognac	कोन्याक (m)	konyāk
rum	रम (m)	ram

coffee	कॉफ़ी (f)	kofī
black coffee	काली कॉफ़ी (f)	kālī kofī
white coffee	दूध के साथ कॉफ़ी (f)	dūdh ke sāth kofī
cappuccino	कैपूचिनो (f)	kaipūchino
instant coffee	इन्सटेन्ट-कॉफ़ी (f)	insatent-kāfī

milk	दूध (m)	dūdh
cocktail	कॉकटेल (m)	kokatel
milkshake	मिल्कशेक (m)	milkashek
juice	रस (m)	ras

tomato juice	टमाटर का रस (m)	tamātar ka ras
orange juice	संतरे का रस (m)	santare ka ras
freshly squeezed juice	ताज़ा रस (m)	tāza ras

beer	बियर (m)	biyar
lager	हल्का बियर (m)	halka biyar
bitter	डार्क बियर (m)	dārk biyar

tea	चाय (f)	chāy
black tea	काली चाय (f)	kālī chāy
green tea	हरी चाय (f)	harī chāy

54. Vegetables

| vegetables | सब्ज़ियाँ (f pl) | sabziyān |
| greens | हरी सब्ज़ियाँ (f) | harī sabziyān |

tomato	टमाटर (m)	tamātar
cucumber	खीरा (m)	khīra
carrot	गाजर (f)	gājar
potato	आलू (m)	ālū
onion	प्याज़ (m)	pyāz
garlic	लहसुन (m)	lahasun

| cabbage | पत्ता गोभी (f) | patta gobhī |
| cauliflower | फूल गोभी (f) | fūl gobhī |

| Brussels sprouts | ब्रसेल्स स्प्राउट्स (m) | brasels sprauts |
| broccoli | ब्रोकोली (f) | brokolī |

beetroot	चुकन्दर (m)	chukandar
aubergine	बैंगन (m)	baingan
courgette	तुरई (f)	turī

| pumpkin | कद्दू | kaddū |
| turnip | शलजम (f) | shalajam |

parsley	अजमोद (f)	ajamod
dill	सोआ (m)	soa
lettuce	सलाद पत्ता (m)	salād patta
celery	सेलरी (m)	selarī

| asparagus | एस्पैरेगस (m) | espairegas |
| spinach | पालक (m) | pālak |

| pea | मटर (m) | matar |
| beans | फली (f pl) | falī |

| maize | मकई (f) | makī |
| kidney bean | राजमा (f) | rājama |

sweet paper	शिमला मिर्च (m)	shimala mirch
radish	मूली (f)	mūlī
artichoke	हाथीचक (m)	hāthīchak

55. Fruits. Nuts

fruit	फल (m)	fal
apple	सेब (m)	seb
pear	नाशपाती (f)	nāshapātī
lemon	नींबू (m)	nīmbū
orange	संतरा (m)	santara
strawberry (garden ~)	स्ट्रॉबेरी (f)	stroberī
tangerine	नारंगी (m)	nārangī
plum	आलूबुखारा (m)	ālūbukhāra
peach	आड़ू (m)	āṛū
apricot	खूबानी (f)	khūbānī
raspberry	रसभरी (f)	rasabharī
pineapple	अनानास (m)	anānās
banana	केला (m)	kela
watermelon	तरबूज़ (m)	tarabūz
grape	अंगूर (m)	angūr
cherry	चेरी (f)	cherī
melon	खरबूज़ा (f)	kharabūza
grapefruit	ग्रेपफ्रूट (m)	grepafrūt
avocado	एवोकाडो (m)	evokādo
papaya	पपीता (f)	papīta
mango	आम (m)	ām
pomegranate	अनार (m)	anār
redcurrant	लाल किशमिश (f)	lāl kishamish
blackcurrant	काली किशमिश (f)	kālī kishamish
gooseberry	आमला (f)	āmala
bilberry	बिलबेरी (f)	bilaberī
blackberry	ब्लैकबेरी (f)	blaikaberī
raisin	किशमिश (m)	kishamish
fig	अंजीर (m)	anjīr
date	खजूर (m)	khajūr
peanut	मूँगफली (m)	mūngafalī
almond	बादाम (f)	bādām
walnut	अखरोट (m)	akharot
hazelnut	हेज़लनट (m)	hezalanat
coconut	नारियल (m)	nāriyal
pistachios	पिस्ता (m)	pista

56. Bread. Sweets

bakers' confectionery (pastry)	मिठाई (f pl)	mithaī
bread	ब्रेड (f)	bred
biscuits	बिस्कुट (m)	biskut
chocolate (n)	चॉकलेट (m)	chokalet
chocolate (as adj)	चॉकलेटी	chokaletī

candy (wrapped)	टॉफ़ी (f)	tofī
cake (e.g. cupcake)	पेस्ट्री (f)	pestrī
cake (e.g. birthday ~)	केक (m)	kek
pie (e.g. apple ~)	पाई (m)	paī
filling (for cake, pie)	फ़िलिंग (f)	filing
jam (whole fruit jam)	जैम (m)	jaim
marmalade	मुरब्बा (m)	murabba
wafers	वेफ़र (m pl)	vefar
ice-cream	आईस-क्रीम (f)	āīs-krīm

57. Spices

salt	नमक (m)	namak
salty (adj)	नमकीन	namakīn
to salt (vt)	नमक डालना	namak dālana
black pepper	काली मिर्च (f)	kālī mirch
red pepper (milled ~)	लाल मिर्च (m)	lāl mirch
mustard	सरसों (m)	sarason
horseradish	अरब मूली (f)	arab mūlī
condiment	मसाला (m)	masāla
spice	मसाला (m)	masāla
sauce	चटनी (f)	chatanī
vinegar	सिरका (m)	siraka
anise	सौंफ़ (f)	saumf
basil	तुलसी (f)	tulasī
cloves	लौंग (f)	laung
ginger	अदरक (m)	adarak
coriander	धनिया (m)	dhaniya
cinnamon	दालचीनी (f)	dālachīnī
sesame	तिल (m)	til
bay leaf	तेजपत्ता (m)	tejapatta
paprika	लाल शिमला मिर्च पाउडर (m)	lāl shimala mirch paudar
caraway	ज़ीरा (m)	zīra
saffron	ज़ाफ़रान (m)	zāfarān

PERSONAL INFORMATION. FAMILY

58. Personal information. Forms

name (first name)	पहला नाम (m)	pahala nām
surname (last name)	उपनाम (m)	upanām
date of birth	जन्म-दिवस (m)	janm-divas
place of birth	मातृभूमि (f)	mātrbhūmi
nationality	नागरिकता (f)	nāgarikata
place of residence	निवास स्थान (m)	nivās sthān
country	देश (m)	desh
profession (occupation)	पेशा (m)	pesha
gender, sex	लिंग (m)	ling
height	क़द (m)	qad
weight	वज़न (m)	vazan

59. Family members. Relatives

mother	माँ (f)	mān
father	पिता (m)	pita
son	बेटा (m)	beta
daughter	बेटी (f)	betī
younger daughter	छोटी बेटी (f)	chhotī betī
younger son	छोटा बेटा (m)	chhota beta
eldest daughter	बड़ी बेटी (f)	barī betī
eldest son	बड़ा बेटा (m)	bara beta
brother	भाई (m)	bhaī
sister	बहन (f)	bahan
cousin (masc.)	चचेरा भाई (m)	chachera bhaī
cousin (fem.)	चचेरी बहन (f)	chacherī bahan
mummy	अम्मा (f)	amma
dad, daddy	पापा (m)	pāpa
parents	माँ-बाप (m pl)	mān-bāp
child	बच्चा (m)	bachcha
children	बच्चे (m pl)	bachche
grandmother	दादी (f)	dādī
grandfather	दादा (m)	dāda
grandson	पोता (m)	pota
granddaughter	पोती (f)	potī
grandchildren	पोते (m)	pote
uncle	चाचा (m)	chācha
aunt	चाची (f)	chāchī

nephew	भतीजा (m)	bhatīja
niece	भतीजी (f)	bhatījī
mother-in-law (wife's mother)	सास (f)	sās
father-in-law (husband's father)	ससुर (m)	sasur
son-in-law (daughter's husband)	दामाद (m)	dāmād
stepmother	सौतेली माँ (f)	sautelī mān
stepfather	सौतेले पिता (m)	sautele pita
infant	दूधमुँहा बच्चा (m)	dudhamunha bachcha
baby (infant)	शिशु (f)	shishu
little boy, kid	छोटा बच्चा (m)	chhota bachcha
wife	पत्नी (f)	patnī
husband	पति (m)	pati
spouse (husband)	पति (m)	pati
spouse (wife)	पत्नी (f)	patnī
married (masc.)	शादीशुदा	shādīshuda
married (fem.)	शादीशुदा	shādīshuda
single (unmarried)	अविवाहित	avivāhit
bachelor	कुँआरा (m)	kunāra
divorced (masc.)	तलाक़शुदा	talāqashuda
widow	विधवा (f)	vidhava
widower	विधुर (m)	vidhur
relative	रिश्तेदार (m)	rishtedār
close relative	सम्बंधी (m)	sambandhī
distant relative	दूर का रिश्तेदार (m)	dūr ka rishtedār
relatives	रिश्तेदार (m pl)	rishtedār
orphan (boy or girl)	अनाथ (m)	anāth
guardian (of a minor)	अभिभावक (m)	abhibhāvak
to adopt (a boy)	लड़का गोद लेना	laraka god lena
to adopt (a girl)	लड़की गोद लेना	larakī god lena

60. Friends. Colleagues

friend (masc.)	दोस्त (m)	dost
friend (fem.)	सहेली (f)	sahelī
friendship	दोस्ती (f)	dostī
to be friends	दोस्त होना	dost hona
pal (masc.)	मित्र (m)	mitr
pal (fem.)	सहेली (f)	sahelī
partner	पार्टनर (m)	pārtanar
chief (boss)	चीफ़ (m)	chīf
superior (n)	अधीक्षक (m)	adhīkshak
subordinate (n)	अधीनस्थ (m)	adhīnasth
colleague	सहकर्मी (m)	sahakarmī

acquaintance (person)	परिचित आदमी (m)	parichit ādamī
fellow traveller	सहगामी (m)	sahagāmī
classmate	सहपाठी (m)	sahapāthī
neighbour (masc.)	पड़ोसी (m)	parosī
neighbour (fem.)	पड़ोसन (f)	parosan
neighbours	पड़ोसी (m pl)	parosī

HUMAN BODY. MEDICINE

61. Head

head	सिर (m)	sir
face	चेहरा (m)	chehara
nose	नाक (f)	nāk
mouth	मुँह (m)	munh
eye	आँख (f)	ānkh
eyes	आँखें (f)	ānkhen
pupil	आँख की पुतली (f)	ānkh kī putalī
eyebrow	भौंह (f)	bhaunh
eyelash	बरौनी (f)	baraunī
eyelid	पलक (m)	palak
tongue	जीभ (m)	jībh
tooth	दाँत (f)	dānt
lips	होंठ (m)	honth
cheekbones	गाल की हड्डी (f)	gāl kī haddī
gum	मसूड़ा (m)	masūra
palate	तालु (m)	tālu
nostrils	नथने (m pl)	nathane
chin	ठोड़ी (f)	thorī
jaw	जबड़ा (m)	jabara
cheek	गाल (m)	gāl
forehead	माथा (m)	mātha
temple	कनपट्टी (f)	kanapattī
ear	कान (m)	kān
back of the head	सिर का पिछला हिस्सा (m)	sir ka pichhala hissa
neck	गरदन (m)	garadan
throat	गला (m)	gala
hair	बाल (m pl)	bāl
hairstyle	हेयरस्टाइल (m)	heyarastail
haircut	हेयरकट (m)	heyarakat
wig	नकली बाल (m)	nakalī bāl
moustache	मूँछें (f pl)	mūnchhen
beard	दाढ़ी (f)	dārhī
to have (a beard, etc.)	होना	hona
plait	चोटी (f)	chotī
sideboards	गलमुच्छा (m)	galamuchchha
red-haired (adj)	लाल बाल	lāl bāl
grey (hair)	सफ़ेद बाल	safed bāl
bald (adj)	गंजा	ganja
bald patch	गंजाई (f)	ganjaī

| ponytail | पोनी-टेल (f) | ponī-tel |
| fringe | बेंग (m) | beng |

62. Human body

hand	हाथ (m)	hāth
arm	बाँह (m)	bānh
finger	उँगली (m)	ungalī
thumb	अँगूठा (m)	angūtha
little finger	छोटी उंगली (f)	chhotī ungalī
nail	नाख़ून (m)	nākhūn
fist	मुट्ठी (m)	mutthī
palm	हथेली (f)	hathelī
wrist	कलाई (f)	kalaī
forearm	प्रकोष्ठ (m)	prakoshth
elbow	कोहनी (f)	kohanī
shoulder	कंधा (m)	kandha
leg	टाँग (f)	tāng
foot	पैर का तलवा (m)	pair ka talava
knee	घुटना (m)	ghutana
calf	पिंडली (f)	pindalī
hip	जाँघ (f)	jāngh
heel	एड़ी (f)	erī
body	शरीर (m)	sharīr
stomach	पेट (m)	pet
chest	सीना (m)	sīna
breast	स्तन (f)	stan
flank	कूल्हा (m)	kūlha
back	पीठ (f)	pīth
lower back	पीठ का निचला हिस्सा (m)	pīth ka nichala hissa
waist	कमर (f)	kamar
navel (belly button)	नाभी (f)	nābhī
buttocks	नितंब (m pl)	nitamb
bottom	नितम्ब (m)	nitamb
beauty spot	सौंदर्य चिन्ह (f)	saundary chinh
birthmark (café au lait spot)	जन्म चिह्न (m)	janm chihn
tattoo	टैट्टू (m)	taitū
scar	घाव का निशान (m)	ghāv ka nishān

63. Diseases

illness	बीमारी (f)	bīmārī
to be ill	बीमार होना	bīmār hona
health	सेहत (f)	sehat
runny nose (coryza)	नज़ला (m)	nazala
tonsillitis	टॉन्सिल (m)	tonsil

cold (illness)	जुकाम (f)	zukām
to catch a cold	जुकाम हो जाना	zukām ho jāna
bronchitis	ब्रॉन्काइटिस (m)	bronkaitis
pneumonia	निमोनिया (f)	nimoniya
flu, influenza	फ्लू (m)	flū
shortsighted (adj)	कमबीन	kamabīn
longsighted (adj)	कमज़ोर दूरदृष्टि	kamazor dūradrshti
strabismus (crossed eyes)	तिरछी नज़र (m)	tirachhī nazar
squint-eyed (adj)	तिरछी नज़रवाला	tirachhī nazaravāla
cataract	मोतिया बिंद (m)	motiya bind
glaucoma	काला मोतिया (m)	kāla motiya
stroke	स्ट्रोक (m)	strok
heart attack	दिल का दौरा (m)	dil ka daura
myocardial infarction	मायोकार्डियल इन्फार्क्शन (m)	māyokārdiyal infārkshan
paralysis	लकवा (m)	lakava
to paralyse (vt)	लक़वा मारना	laqava mārana
allergy	एलर्जी (f)	elarjī
asthma	दमा (f)	dama
diabetes	शूगर (f)	shūgar
toothache	दाँत दर्द (m)	dānt dard
caries	दाँत में कीड़ा (m)	dānt men kīra
diarrhoea	दस्त (m)	dast
constipation	कब्ज़ (m)	kabz
stomach upset	पेट ख़राब (m)	pet kharāb
food poisoning	ख़राब खाने से हुई बीमारी (f)	kharāb khāne se huī bīmārī
to get food poisoning	ख़राब खाने से बीमार पड़ना	kharāb khāne se bīmār parana
arthritis	गठिया (m)	gathiya
rickets	बालवक्र (m)	bālavakr
rheumatism	आमवात (m)	āmavāt
atherosclerosis	धमनीकलाकाठिन्य (m)	dhamanīkalākāthiny
gastritis	जठर-शोथ (m)	jathar-shoth
appendicitis	उण्डुक-शोथ (m)	unduk-shoth
cholecystitis	पित्ताशय (m)	pittāshay
ulcer	अल्सर (m)	alsar
measles	मीज़ल्स (m)	mīzals
rubella (German measles)	जर्मन मीज़ल्स (m)	jarman mīzals
jaundice	पीलिया (m)	pīliya
hepatitis	हेपेटाइटिस (m)	hepetaitis
schizophrenia	शीज़ोफ्रेनीय (f)	shīzofrenīy
rabies (hydrophobia)	रेबीज़ (m)	rebīz
neurosis	न्यूरोसिस (m)	nyūrosis
concussion	आघात (m)	āghāt
cancer	कर्क रोग (m)	kark rog
sclerosis	काठिन्य (m)	kāthiny

multiple sclerosis	मल्टीपल स्क्लेरोसिस (m)	maltīpal sclerosis
alcoholism	शराबीपन (m)	sharābīpan
alcoholic (n)	शराबी (m)	sharābī
syphilis	सीफ़िलिस (m)	sīfilis
AIDS	ऐड्स (m)	aids

tumour	ट्यूमर (m)	tyūmar
malignant (adj)	घातक	ghātak
benign (adj)	अर्बुद	arbud

fever	बुख़ार (m)	bukhār
malaria	मलेरिया (f)	maleriya
gangrene	गैन्ग्रीन (m)	gaingrīn
seasickness	जहाज़ी मतली (f)	jahāzī matalī
epilepsy	मिरगी (f)	miragī

epidemic	महामारी (f)	mahāmārī
typhus	टाइफ़स (m)	taifas
tuberculosis	टीबी (m)	tībī
cholera	हैज़ा (f)	haiza
plague (bubonic ~)	प्लेग (f)	pleg

64. Symptoms. Treatments. Part 1

symptom	लक्षण (m)	lakshan
temperature	तापमान (m)	tāpamān
high temperature (fever)	बुख़ार (f)	bukhār
pulse (heartbeat)	नब्ज़ (f)	nabz

dizziness (vertigo)	सिर का चक्कर (m)	sir ka chakkar
hot (adj)	गरम	garam
shivering	कंपकंपी (f)	kampakampī
pale (e.g. ~ face)	पीला	pīla

cough	खाँसी (f)	khānsī
to cough (vi)	खाँसना	khānsana
to sneeze (vi)	छींकना	chhīnkana
faint	बेहोशी (f)	behoshī
to faint (vi)	बेहोश होना	behosh hona

bruise (hématome)	नील (m)	nīl
bump (lump)	गुमड़ा (m)	gumara
to bang (bump)	चोट लगना	chot lagana
contusion (bruise)	चोट (f)	chot
to get a bruise	घाव लगना	ghāv lagana

to limp (vi)	लँगड़ाना	langarāna
dislocation	हड्डी खिसकना (f)	haddī khisakana
to dislocate (vt)	हड्डी खिसकना	haddī khisakana
fracture	हड्डी टूट जाना (f)	haddī tūt jāna
to have a fracture	हड्डी टूट जाना	haddī tūt jāna

| cut (e.g. paper ~) | कट जाना (m) | kat jāna |
| to cut oneself | ख़ुद को काट लेना | khud ko kāt lena |

bleeding	रक्त-स्राव (m)	rakt-srāv
burn (injury)	जला होना	jala hona
to get burned	जल जाना	jal jāna

to prick (vt)	चुभाना	chubhāna
to prick oneself	खुद को चुभाना	khud ko chubhāna
to injure (vt)	घायल करना	ghāyal karana
injury	चोट (f)	chot
wound	घाव (m)	ghāv
trauma	चोट (f)	chot

to be delirious	बेहोशी में बड़बड़ाना	behoshī men barabadāna
to stutter (vi)	हकलाना	hakalāna
sunstroke	धूप आघात (m)	dhūp āghāt

65. Symptoms. Treatments. Part 2

| pain, ache | दर्द (f) | dard |
| splinter (in foot, etc.) | चुभ जाना (m) | chubh jāna |

sweat (perspiration)	पसीना (f)	pasīna
to sweat (perspire)	पसीना निकलना	pasīna nikalana
vomiting	वमन (m)	vaman
convulsions	दौरा (m)	daura

pregnant (adj)	गर्भवती	garbhavatī
to be born	जन्म लेना	janm lena
delivery, labour	पैदा करना (m)	paida karana
to deliver (~ a baby)	पैदा करना	paida karana
abortion	गर्भपात (m)	garbhapāt

breathing, respiration	साँस (f)	sāns
in-breath (inhalation)	साँस अंदर खींचना (f)	sāns andar khīnchana
out-breath (exhalation)	साँस बाहर छोड़ना (f)	sāns bāhar chhorana
to exhale (breathe out)	साँस बाहर छोड़ना	sāns bāhar chhorana
to inhale (vi)	साँस अंदर खींचना	sāns andar khīnchana

disabled person	अपाहिज (m)	apāhij
cripple	लूला (m)	lūla
drug addict	नशेबाज़ (m)	nashebāz

deaf (adj)	बहरा	bahara
mute (adj)	गूँगा	gūnga
deaf mute (adj)	बहरा और गूँगा	bahara aur gūnga

mad, insane (adj)	पागल	pāgal
madman (demented person)	पगला (m)	pagala
madwoman	पगली (f)	pagalī
to go insane	पागल हो जाना	pāgal ho jāna

gene	वंशाणु (m)	vanshānu
immunity	रोग प्रतिरोधक शक्ति (f)	rog pratirodhak shakti
hereditary (adj)	जन्मजात	janmajāt

congenital (adj)	पैदाइशी	paidaishī
virus	विषाणु (m)	vishānu
microbe	कीटाणु (m)	kītānu
bacterium	जीवाणु (m)	jīvānu
infection	संक्रमण (m)	sankraman

66. Symptoms. Treatments. Part 3

hospital	अस्पताल (m)	aspatāl
patient	मरीज़ (m)	marīz
diagnosis	रोग-निर्णय (m)	rog-nirnay
cure	इलाज (m)	ilāj
medical treatment	चिकित्सीय उपचार (m)	chikitsīy upachār
to get treatment	इलाज कराना	ilāj karāna
to treat (~ a patient)	इलाज करना	ilāj karana
to nurse (look after)	देखभाल करना	dekhabhāl karana
care (nursing ~)	देखभाल (f)	dekhabhāl
operation, surgery	ऑपरेशन (m)	opareshan
to bandage (head, limb)	पट्टी बाँधना	pattī bāndhana
bandaging	पट्टी (f)	pattī
vaccination	टीका (m)	tīka
to vaccinate (vt)	टीका लगाना	tīka lagāna
injection	इंजेक्शन (m)	injekshan
to give an injection	इंजेक्शन लगाना	injekshan lagāna
amputation	अंगविच्छेद (f)	angavichchhed
to amputate (vt)	अंगविच्छेद करना	angavichchhed karana
coma	कोमा (m)	koma
to be in a coma	कोमा में चले जाना	koma men chale jāna
intensive care	गहन चिकित्सा (f)	gahan chikitsa
to recover (~ from flu)	ठीक हो जाना	thīk ho jāna
condition (patient's ~)	हालत (m)	hālat
consciousness	होश (m)	hosh
memory (faculty)	याददाश्त (f)	yādadāsht
to pull out (tooth)	दाँत निकालना	dānt nikālana
filling	भराव (m)	bharāv
to fill (a tooth)	दाँत को भरना	dānt ko bharana
hypnosis	हिपनोसिस (m)	hipanosis
to hypnotize (vt)	हिपनोटाइज़ करना	hipanotaiz karana

67. Medicine. Drugs. Accessories

medicine, drug	दवा (f)	dava
remedy	दवाई (f)	davaī
to prescribe (vt)	नुस्ख़ा लिखना	nusakha likhana
prescription	नुस्ख़ा (m)	nusakha

tablet, pill	गोली (f)	golī
ointment	मरहम (m)	maraham
ampoule	एम्प्यूल (m)	empyūl
mixture, solution	सिरप (m)	sirap
syrup	शरबत (m)	sharabat
capsule	गोली (f)	golī
powder	चूरन (m)	chūran

gauze bandage	पट्टी (f)	pattī
cotton wool	रूई का गोला (m)	rūī ka gola
iodine	आयोडीन (m)	āyodīn

plaster	बैंड-एड (m)	baind-ed
eyedropper	आई-ड्रॉपर (m)	āī-dropar
thermometer	थरमामीटर (m)	tharamāmītar
syringe	इंजेक्शन (m)	injekshan

| wheelchair | व्हीलचेयर (f) | vhīlacheyar |
| crutches | बैसाखी (m pl) | baisākhī |

painkiller	दर्द-निवारक (f)	dard-nivārak
laxative	जुलाब की गोली (f)	julāb kī golī
spirits (ethanol)	स्पिरिट (m)	spirit
medicinal herbs	जड़ी-बूटी (f)	jarī-būtī
herbal (~ tea)	जड़ी-बूटियों से बना	jarī-būtiyon se bana

FLAT

68. Flat

flat	प्लैट (f)	flait
room	कमरा (m)	kamara
bedroom	सोने का कमरा (m)	sone ka kamara
dining room	खाने का कमरा (m)	khāne ka kamara
living room	बैठक (f)	baithak
study (home office)	घरेलू कार्यालय (m)	gharelū kāryālay
entry room	प्रवेश कक्ष (m)	pravesh kaksh
bathroom	स्नानघर (m)	snānaghar
water closet	शौचालय (m)	shauchālay
ceiling	छत (f)	chhat
floor	फ़र्श (m)	farsh
corner	कोना (m)	kona

69. Furniture. Interior

furniture	फ़र्निचर (m)	farnichar
table	मेज़ (f)	mez
chair	कुर्सी (f)	kursī
bed	पलंग (m)	palang
sofa, settee	सोफ़ा (m)	sofa
armchair	हत्थे वाली कुर्सी (f)	hatthe vālī kursī
bookcase	किताबों की अलमारी (f)	kitābon kī alamārī
shelf	शेल्फ़ (f)	shelf
wardrobe	कपड़ों की अलमारी (f)	kaparon kī alamārī
coat rack (wall-mounted ~)	खूँटी (f)	khūntī
coat stand	खूँटी (f)	khūntī
chest of drawers	कपड़ों की अलमारी (f)	kaparon kī alamārī
coffee table	कॉफ़ी की मेज़ (f)	kofī kī mez
mirror	आईना (m)	āīna
carpet	कालीन (m)	kālīn
small carpet	दरी (f)	darī
fireplace	चिमनी (f)	chimanī
candle	मोमबत्ती (f)	momabattī
candlestick	मोमबत्तीदान (m)	momabattīdān
drapes	परदे (m pl)	parade
wallpaper	वॉल पेपर (m)	vol pepar

blinds (jalousie)	जेलुज़ी (f pl)	jeluzī
table lamp	मेज़ का लैम्प (m)	mez ka laimp
wall lamp (sconce)	दिवार का लैम्प (m)	divār ka laimp
standard lamp	फ़र्श का लैम्प (m)	farsh ka laimp
chandelier	झूमर (m)	jhūmar
leg (of a chair, table)	पाँव (m)	pānv
armrest	कुर्सी का हत्था (m)	kursī ka hattha
back (backrest)	कुर्सी की पीठ (f)	kursī kī pīth
drawer	दराज़ (m)	darāz

70. Bedding

bedclothes	बिस्तर के कपड़े (m)	bistar ke kapare
pillow	तकिया (m)	takiya
pillowslip	ग़िलाफ़ (m)	gilāf
duvet	रज़ाई (f)	razaī
sheet	चादर (f)	chādar
bedspread	चादर (f)	chādar

71. Kitchen

kitchen	रसोईघर (m)	rasoīghar
gas	गैस (m)	gais
gas cooker	गैस का चूल्हा (m)	gais ka chūlha
electric cooker	बिजली का चूल्हा (m)	bijalī ka chūlha
oven	ओवन (m)	ovan
microwave oven	माइक्रोवेव ओवन (m)	maikrovev ovan
refrigerator	फ़्रिज (m)	frij
freezer	फ़्रीजर (m)	frījar
dishwasher	डिशवॉशर (m)	dishavoshar
mincer	कीमा बनाने की मशीन (f)	kīma banāne kī mashīn
juicer	जूसर (m)	jūsar
toaster	टोस्टर (m)	tostar
mixer	मिक्सर (m)	miksar
coffee machine	कॉफ़ी मशीन (f)	kofī mashīn
coffee pot	कॉफ़ी पॉट (m)	kofī pot
coffee grinder	कॉफ़ी पीसने की मशीन (f)	kofī pīsane kī mashīn
kettle	केतली (f)	ketalī
teapot	चायदानी (f)	chāyadānī
lid	ढक्कन (m)	dhakkan
tea strainer	छलनी (f)	chhalanī
spoon	चम्मच (m)	chammach
teaspoon	चम्मच (m)	chammach
soup spoon	चम्मच (m)	chammach
fork	काँटा (m)	kānta
knife	छुरी (f)	chhurī

tableware (dishes)	बरतन (m)	baratan
plate (dinner ~)	तश्तरी (f)	tashtarī
saucer	तश्तरी (f)	tashtarī
shot glass	जाम (m)	jām
glass (tumbler)	गिलास (m)	gilās
cup	प्याला (m)	pyāla
sugar bowl	चीनीदानी (f)	chīnīdānī
salt cellar	नमकदानी (m)	namakadānī
pepper pot	मिर्चदानी (f)	mirchadānī
butter dish	मक्खनदानी (f)	makkhanadānī
stock pot (soup pot)	सॉसपैन (m)	sosapain
frying pan (skillet)	फ्राइ पैन (f)	frai pain
ladle	डोई (f)	doī
colander	कालेन्डर (m)	kālendar
tray (serving ~)	थाली (m)	thālī
bottle	बोतल (f)	botal
jar (glass)	शीशी (f)	shīshī
tin (can)	डिब्बा (m)	dibba
bottle opener	बोतल ओपनर (m)	botal opanar
tin opener	ओपनर (m)	opanar
corkscrew	पेंचकस (m)	penchakas
filter	फ़िल्टर (m)	filtar
to filter (vt)	फ़िल्टर करना	filtar karana
waste (food ~, etc.)	कूड़ा (m)	kūra
waste bin (kitchen ~)	कूड़े की बाल्टी (f)	kūre kī bāltī

72. Bathroom

bathroom	स्नानघर (m)	snānaghar
water	पानी (m)	pānī
tap	नल (m)	nal
hot water	गरम पानी (m)	garam pānī
cold water	ठंडा पानी (m)	thanda pānī
toothpaste	टूथपेस्ट (m)	tūthapest
to clean one's teeth	दांत ब्रश करना	dānt brash karana
to shave (vi)	शेव करना	shev karana
shaving foam	शेविंग फ़्रोम (m)	sheving fom
razor	रेज़र (f)	rezar
to wash (one's hands, etc.)	धोना	dhona
to have a bath	नहाना	nahāna
shower	शावर (m)	shāvar
to have a shower	शावर लेना	shāvar lena
bath	बाथटब (m)	bāthatab
toilet (toilet bowl)	संडास (m)	sandās

sink (washbasin)	सिंक (m)	sink
soap	साबुन (m)	sābun
soap dish	साबुनदानी (f)	sābunadānī
sponge	स्पंज (f)	spanj
shampoo	शैम्पू (m)	shaimpū
towel	तौलिया (f)	tauliya
bathrobe	चोगा (m)	choga
laundry (laundering)	धुलाई (f)	dhulaī
washing machine	वॉशिंग मशीन (f)	voshing mashīn
to do the laundry	कपड़े धोना	kapare dhona
washing powder	कपड़े धोने का पाउडर (m)	kapare dhone ka paudar

73. Household appliances

TV, telly	टीवी सेट (m)	tīvī set
tape recorder	टेप रिकार्डर (m)	tep rikārdar
video	वीडियो टेप रिकार्डर (m)	vīdiyo tep rikārdar
radio	रेडियो (m)	rediyo
player (CD, MP3, etc.)	प्लेयर (m)	pleyar
video projector	वीडियो प्रोजेक्टर (m)	vīdiyo projektar
home cinema	होम थीएटर (m)	hom thīetar
DVD player	डीवीडी प्लेयर (m)	dīvīdī pleyar
amplifier	ध्वनि-विस्तारक (m)	dhvani-vistārak
video game console	वीडियो गेम कन्सोल (m)	vīdiyo gem kansol
video camera	वीडियो कैमरा (m)	vīdiyo kaimara
camera (photo)	कैमरा (m)	kaimara
digital camera	डीजिटल कैमरा (m)	dījital kaimara
vacuum cleaner	वैक्यूम क्लीनर (m)	vaikyūm klīnar
iron (e.g. steam ~)	इस्तरी (f)	istarī
ironing board	इस्तरी तख़्ता (m)	istarī takhta
telephone	टेलीफ़ोन (m)	telīfon
mobile phone	मोबाइल फ़ोन (m)	mobail fon
typewriter	टाइपराइटर (m)	taiparaitar
sewing machine	सिलाई मशीन (f)	silaī mashīn
microphone	माइक्रोफ़ोन (m)	maikrofon
headphones	हैडफ़ोन (m pl)	hairafon
remote control (TV)	रिमोट (m)	rimot
CD, compact disc	सीडी (m)	sīdī
cassette, tape	कैसेट (f)	kaiset
vinyl record	रिकार्ड (m)	rikārd

THE EARTH. WEATHER

74. Outer space

space	अंतरिक्ष (m)	antariksh
space (as adj)	अंतरिक्षीय	antarikshīy
outer space	अंतरिक्ष (m)	antariksh
world, universe	ब्रह्माण्ड (m)	brahmānd
galaxy	आकाशगंगा (f)	ākāshaganga
star	सितारा (m)	sitāra
constellation	नक्षत्र (m)	nakshatr
planet	ग्रह (m)	grah
satellite	उपग्रह (m)	upagrah
meteorite	उल्का पिंड (m)	ulka pind
comet	पुच्छल तारा (m)	puchchhal tāra
asteroid	ग्रहिका (f)	grahika
orbit	ग्रहपथ (m)	grahapath
to revolve	चक्कर लगना	chakkar lagana
(~ around the Earth)		
atmosphere	वातावरण (m)	vātāvaran
the Sun	सूरज (m)	sūraj
solar system	सौर प्रणाली (f)	saur pranālī
solar eclipse	सूर्य ग्रहण (m)	sūry grahan
the Earth	पृथ्वी (f)	prthvī
the Moon	चांद (m)	chānd
Mars	मंगल (m)	mangal
Venus	शुक्र (m)	shukr
Jupiter	बृहस्पति (m)	brhaspati
Saturn	शनि (m)	shani
Mercury	बुध (m)	budh
Uranus	अरुण (m)	arun
Neptune	वरुण (m)	varūn
Pluto	प्लूटो (m)	plūto
Milky Way	आकाश गंगा (f)	ākāsh ganga
Great Bear (Ursa Major)	ससर्षिमंडल (m)	saptarshimandal
North Star	ध्रुव तारा (m)	dhruv tāra
Martian	मंगल ग्रह का निवासी (m)	mangal grah ka nivāsī
extraterrestrial (n)	अन्य नक्षत्र का निवासी (m)	any nakshatr ka nivāsī
alien	अन्य नक्षत्र का निवासी (m)	any nakshatr ka nivāsī
flying saucer	उड़न तश्तरी (f)	uran tashtarī
spaceship	अंतरिक्ष विमान (m)	antariksh vimān

space station	अंतरिक्ष अड्डा (m)	antariksh adda
blast-off	चालू करना (m)	chālū karana
engine	इंजन (m)	injan
nozzle	नोज़ल (m)	nozal
fuel	ईंधन (m)	īndhan
cockpit, flight deck	केबिन (m)	kebin
aerial	एरियल (m)	eriyal
porthole	विमान गवाक्ष (m)	vimān gavāksh
solar panel	सौर पेनल (m)	saur penal
spacesuit	अंतरिक्ष पोशाक (m)	antariksh poshāk
weightlessness	भारहीनता (m)	bhārahīnata
oxygen	आक्सीजन (m)	āksījan
docking (in space)	डॉकिंग (f)	doking
to dock (vi, vt)	डॉकिंग करना	doking karana
observatory	वेधशाला (m)	vedhashāla
telescope	दूरबीन (f)	dūrabīn
to observe (vt)	देखना	dekhana
to explore (vt)	जाँचना	jānchana

75. The Earth

the Earth	पृथ्वी (f)	prthvī
the globe (the Earth)	गोला (m)	gola
planet	ग्रह (m)	grah
atmosphere	वातावरण (m)	vātāvaran
geography	भूगोल (m)	bhūgol
nature	प्रकृति (f)	prakrti
globe (table ~)	गोलक (m)	golak
map	नक्शा (m)	naksha
atlas	मानचित्रावली (f)	mānachitrāvalī
Europe	यूरोप (m)	yūrop
Asia	एशिया (f)	eshiya
Africa	अफ्रीका (m)	afrīka
Australia	ऑस्ट्रेलिया (m)	ostreliya
America	अमेरिका (f)	amerika
North America	उत्तरी अमेरिका (f)	uttarī amerika
South America	दक्षिणी अमेरिका (f)	dakshinī amerika
Antarctica	अंटार्कटिक (m)	antārkatik
the Arctic	आर्कटिक (m)	ārkatik

76. Cardinal directions

north	उत्तर (m)	uttar
to the north	उत्तर की ओर	uttar kī or

| in the north | उत्तर में | uttar men |
| northern (adj) | उत्तरी | uttarī |

south	दक्षिण (m)	dakshin
to the south	दक्षिण की ओर	dakshin kī or
in the south	दक्षिण में	dakshin men
southern (adj)	दक्षिणी	dakshinī

west	पश्चिम (m)	pashchim
to the west	पश्चिम की ओर	pashchim kī or
in the west	पश्चिम में	pashchim men
western (adj)	पश्चिमी	pashchimī

east	पूर्व (m)	pūrv
to the east	पूर्व की ओर	pūrv kī or
in the east	पूर्व में	pūrv men
eastern (adj)	पूर्वी	pūrvī

77. Sea. Ocean

sea	सागर (m)	sāgar
ocean	महासागर (m)	mahāsāgar
gulf (bay)	खाड़ी (f)	khārī
straits	जलग्रीवा (m)	jalagrīva

continent (mainland)	महाद्वीप (m)	mahādvīp
island	द्वीप (m)	dvīp
peninsula	प्रायद्वीप (m)	prāyadvīp
archipelago	द्वीप समूह (m)	dvīp samūh

bay, cove	तट-खाड़ी (f)	tat-khārī
harbour	बंदरगाह (m)	bandaragāh
lagoon	लैगून (m)	laigūn
cape	अंतरीप (m)	antarīp

atoll	एटोल (m)	etol
reef	रीफ़ (m)	rīf
coral	प्रवाल (m)	pravāl
coral reef	प्रवाल रीफ़ (m)	pravāl rīf

deep (adj)	गहरा	gahara
depth (deep water)	गहराई (f)	gaharaī
abyss	रसातल (m)	rasātal
trench (e.g. Mariana ~)	गड्ढा (m)	garha

| current (Ocean ~) | धारा (f) | dhāra |
| to surround (bathe) | घिरा होना | ghira hona |

| shore | किनारा (m) | kināra |
| coast | तटबंध (m) | tatabandh |

flow (flood tide)	ज्वार (m)	jvār
ebb (ebb tide)	भाटा (m)	bhāta
shoal	रेती (m)	retī

bottom (~ of the sea)	तला (m)	tala
wave	तरंग (f)	tarang
crest (~ of a wave)	तरंग शिखर (f)	tarang shikhar
spume (sea foam)	झाग (m)	jhāg
hurricane	तूफ़ान (m)	tufān
tsunami	सुनामी (f)	sunāmī
calm (dead ~)	शांत (m)	shānt
quiet, calm (adj)	शांत	shānt
pole	ध्रुव (m)	dhruv
polar (adj)	ध्रुवीय	dhruvīy
latitude	अक्षांश (m)	akshānsh
longitude	देशान्तर (m)	deshāntar
parallel	समांतर-रेखा (f)	samāntar-rekha
equator	भूमध्य रेखा (f)	bhūmadhy rekha
sky	आकाश (f)	ākāsh
horizon	क्षितिज (m)	kshitij
air	हवा (f)	hava
lighthouse	प्रकाशस्तंभ (m)	prakāshastambh
to dive (vi)	गोता मारना	gota mārana
to sink (ab. boat)	डूब जाना	dūb jāna
treasure	ख़ज़ाना (m)	khazāna

78. Seas & Oceans names

Atlantic Ocean	अटलांटिक महासागर (m)	atalāntik mahāsāgar
Indian Ocean	हिन्द महासागर (m)	hind mahāsāgar
Pacific Ocean	प्रशांत महासागर (m)	prashānt mahāsāgar
Arctic Ocean	उत्तरी ध्रुव महासागर (m)	uttarī dhuv mahāsāgar
Black Sea	काला सागर (m)	kāla sāgar
Red Sea	लाल सागर (m)	lāl sāgar
Yellow Sea	पीला सागर (m)	pīla sāgar
White Sea	सफ़ेद सागर (m)	safed sāgar
Caspian Sea	कैस्पियन सागर (m)	kaispiyan sāgar
Dead Sea	मृत सागर (m)	mrt sāgar
Mediterranean Sea	भूमध्य सागर (m)	bhūmadhy sāgar
Aegean Sea	ईजियन सागर (m)	ījiyan sāgar
Adriatic Sea	एड्रिएटिक सागर (m)	edrietik sāgar
Arabian Sea	अरब सागर (m)	arab sāgar
Sea of Japan	जापान सागर (m)	jāpān sāgar
Bering Sea	बेरिंग सागर (m)	bering sāgar
South China Sea	दक्षिण चीन सागर (m)	dakshin chīn sāgar
Coral Sea	कोरल सागर (m)	koral sāgar
Tasman Sea	तस्मान सागर (m)	tasmān sāgar
Caribbean Sea	करिबियन सागर (m)	karibiyan sāgar

Barents Sea	बैरेंट्स सागर (m)	bairents sāgar
Kara Sea	काड़ा सागर (m)	kāra sāgar
North Sea	उत्तर सागर (m)	uttar sāgar
Baltic Sea	बाल्टिक सागर (m)	bāltik sāgar
Norwegian Sea	नार्वे सागर (m)	nārve sāgar

79. Mountains

mountain	पहाड़ (m)	pahār
mountain range	पर्वत माला (f)	parvat māla
mountain ridge	पहाड़ों का सिलसिला (m)	pahāron ka silasila
summit, top	चोटी (f)	chotī
peak	शिखर (m)	shikhar
foot (~ of the mountain)	तलहटी (f)	talahatī
slope (mountainside)	ढलान (f)	dhalān
volcano	ज्वालामुखी (m)	jvālāmukhī
active volcano	सक्रिय ज्वालामुखी (m)	sakriy jvālāmukhī
dormant volcano	निष्क्रिय ज्वालामुखी (m)	nishkriy jvālāmukhī
eruption	विस्फोटन (m)	visfotan
crater	ज्वालामुखी का मुख (m)	jvālāmukhī ka mukh
magma	मैग्मा (m)	maigma
lava	लावा (m)	lāva
molten (~ lava)	पिघला हुआ	pighala hua
canyon	घाटी (m)	ghātī
gorge	तंग घाटी (f)	tang ghātī
crevice	दरार (m)	darār
pass, col	मार्ग (m)	mārg
plateau	पठार (m)	pathār
cliff	शिला (f)	shila
hill	टीला (m)	tīla
glacier	हिमनद (m)	himanad
waterfall	झरना (m)	jharana
geyser	उष्ण जल स्रोत (m)	ushn jal srot
lake	तालाब (m)	tālāb
plain	समतल प्रदेश (m)	samatal pradesh
landscape	परिदृश्य (m)	paridrshy
echo	गूँज (f)	gūnj
alpinist	पर्वतारोही (m)	parvatārohī
rock climber	पर्वतारोही (m)	parvatārohī
to conquer (in climbing)	चोटी पर पहुँचना	chotī par pahunchana
climb (an easy ~)	चढ़ाव (m)	charhāv

80. Mountains names

The Alps	आल्पस (m)	ālpas
Mont Blanc	मोन्ट ब्लैंक (m)	mont blaink
The Pyrenees	पाइरीनीज़ (f pl)	pairīnīz

The Carpathians	कार्पाथियेन्स (m)	kārpāthiyens
The Ural Mountains	यूरल (m)	yūral
The Caucasus Mountains	कोकेशिया के पहाड़ (m)	kokeshiya ke pahār
Mount Elbrus	एल्ब्रस पर्वत (m)	elbras parvat

The Altai Mountains	अल्टाई पर्वत (m)	altaī parvat
The Tian Shan	तियान शान (m)	tiyān shān
The Pamirs	पामीर पर्वत (m)	pāmīr parvat
The Himalayas	हिमालय (m)	himālay
Mount Everest	माउंट एवरेस्ट (m)	maunt evarest

| The Andes | एंडीज़ (f pl) | endīz |
| Mount Kilimanjaro | किलीमन्जारो (m) | kilīmanjāro |

81. Rivers

river	नदी (f)	nadī
spring (natural source)	झरना (m)	jharana
riverbed (river channel)	नदी तल (m)	nadī tal
basin (river valley)	बेसिन (m)	besin
to flow into ...	गिरना	girana

| tributary | उपनदी (f) | upanadī |
| bank (river ~) | तट (m) | tat |

current (stream)	धारा (f)	dhāra
downstream (adv)	बहाव के साथ	bahāv ke sāth
upstream (adv)	बहाव के विरुद्ध	bahāv ke virūddh

inundation	बाढ़ (f)	bārh
flooding	बाढ़ (f)	bārh
to overflow (vi)	उमड़ना	umarana
to flood (vt)	पानी से भरना	pānī se bharana

| shallow (shoal) | छिछला पानी (m) | chhichhala pānī |
| rapids | तेज़ उतार (m) | tez utār |

dam	बांध (m)	bāndh
canal	नहर (f)	nahar
reservoir (artificial lake)	जलाशय (m)	jalāshay
sluice, lock	स्लूस (m)	slūs

water body (pond, etc.)	जल स्रोत (m)	jal srot
swamp (marshland)	दलदल (f)	daladal
bog, marsh	दलदल (f)	daladal
whirlpool	भंवर (m)	bhanvar
stream (brook)	झरना (m)	jharana

drinking (ab. water)	पीने का	pīne ka
fresh (~ water)	ताज़ा	tāza
ice	बर्फ़ (m)	barf
to freeze over (ab. river, etc.)	जम जाना	jam jāna

82. Rivers names

Seine	सीन (f)	sīn
Loire	लॉयर (f)	loyar
Thames	थेम्स (f)	thems
Rhine	राइन (f)	rain
Danube	डेन्यूब (f)	denyūb
Volga	वोल्गा (f)	volga
Don	डॉन (f)	don
Lena	लेना (f)	lena
Yellow River	ह्वांग हे (f)	hvāng he
Yangtze	यांग्त्ज़ी (f)	yāngtzī
Mekong	मेकांग (f)	mekāng
Ganges	गंगा (f)	ganga
Nile River	नील (f)	nīl
Congo River	कांगो (f)	kāngo
Okavango River	ओकावान्गो (f)	okāvāngo
Zambezi River	ज़म्बेज़ी (f)	zambezī
Limpopo River	लिम्पोपो (f)	limpopo
Mississippi River	मिसिसिपी (f)	misisipī

83. Forest

forest, wood	जंगल (m)	jangal
forest (as adj)	जंगली	jangalī
thick forest	घना जंगल (m)	ghana jangal
grove	उपवान (m)	upavān
forest clearing	खुला छोटा मैदान (m)	khula chhota maidān
thicket	झाड़ियाँ (f pl)	jhāriyān
scrubland	झाड़ियों भरा मैदान (m)	jhāriyon bhara maidān
footpath (troddenpath)	फुटपाथ (m)	futapāth
gully	नाली (f)	nālī
tree	पेड़ (m)	per
leaf	पत्ता (m)	patta
leaves (foliage)	पत्तियां (f)	pattiyān
fall of leaves	पतझड़ (m)	patajhar
to fall (ab. leaves)	गिरना	girana

top (of the tree)	शिखर (m)	shikhar
branch	टहनी (f)	tahanī
bough	शाखा (f)	shākha
bud (on shrub, tree)	कलिका (f)	kalika
needle (of the pine tree)	सुई (f)	suī
fir cone	शंकुफल (m)	shankufal
tree hollow	खोखला (m)	khokhala
nest	घोंसला (m)	ghonsala
burrow (animal hole)	बिल (m)	bil
trunk	तना (m)	tana
root	जड़ (f)	jar
bark	छाल (f)	chhāl
moss	काई (f)	kaī
to uproot (remove trees or tree stumps)	उखाड़ना	ukhārana
to chop down	काटना	kātana
to deforest (vt)	जंगल काटना	jangal kātana
tree stump	ठूंठ (m)	thūnth
campfire	अलाव (m)	alāv
forest fire	जंगल की आग (f)	jangal kī āg
to extinguish (vt)	आग बुझाना	āg bujhāna
forest ranger	वनरक्षक (m)	vanarakshak
protection	रक्षा (f)	raksha
to protect (~ nature)	रक्षा करना	raksha karana
poacher	चोर शिकारी (m)	chor shikārī
steel trap	फंदा (m)	fanda
to gather, to pick (vt)	बटोरना	batorana
to lose one's way	रास्ता भूलना	rāsta bhūlana

84. Natural resources

natural resources	प्राकृतिक संसाधन (m pl)	prākrtik sansādhan
minerals	खनिज पदार्थ (m pl)	khanij padārth
deposits	तह (f pl)	tah
field (e.g. oilfield)	क्षेत्र (m)	kshetr
to mine (extract)	खोदना	khodana
mining (extraction)	खनिकर्म (m)	khanikarm
ore	अयस्क (m)	ayask
mine (e.g. for coal)	खान (f)	khān
shaft (mine ~)	शैफ़्ट (m)	shaifat
miner	खनिक (m)	khanik
gas (natural ~)	गैस (m)	gais
gas pipeline	गैस पाइप लाइन (m)	gais paip lain
oil (petroleum)	पेट्रोल (m)	petrol
oil pipeline	तेल पाइप लाइन (m)	tel paip lain

oil well	तेल का कुँआ (m)	tel ka kuna
derrick (tower)	डेरिक (m)	derik
tanker	टैंकर (m)	tainkar

sand	रेत (m)	ret
limestone	चूना पत्थर (m)	chūna patthar
gravel	बजरी (f)	bajarī
peat	पीट (m)	pīt
clay	मिट्टी (f)	mittī
coal	कोयला (m)	koyala

iron (ore)	लोहा (m)	loha
gold	सोना (m)	sona
silver	चाँदी (f)	chāndī
nickel	गिलट (m)	gilat
copper	ताँबा (m)	tānba

zinc	जस्ता (m)	jasta
manganese	अयस (m)	ayas
mercury	पारा (f)	pāra
lead	सीसा (f)	sīsa

mineral	खनिज (m)	khanij
crystal	क्रिस्टल (m)	kristal
marble	संगमरमर (m)	sangamaramar
uranium	यूरेनियम (m)	yūreniyam

85. Weather

weather	मौसम (m)	mausam
weather forecast	मौसम का पूर्वानुमान (m)	mausam ka pūrvānumān
temperature	तापमान (m)	tāpamān
thermometer	थर्मामीटर (m)	tharmāmītar
barometer	बैरोमीटर (m)	bairomītar

humidity	नमी (f)	namī
heat (extreme ~)	गरमी (f)	garamī
hot (torrid)	गरम	garam
it's hot	गरमी है	garamī hai

| it's warm | गरम है | garam hai |
| warm (moderately hot) | गरम | garam |

| it's cold | ठंडक है | thandak hai |
| cold (adj) | ठंडा | thanda |

sun	सूरज (m)	sūraj
to shine (vi)	चमकना	chamakana
sunny (day)	धूपदार	dhūpadār
to come up (vi)	उगना	ugana
to set (vi)	डूबना	dūbana

| cloud | बादल (m) | bādal |
| cloudy (adj) | मेघाच्छादित | meghāchchhādit |

| rain cloud | घना बादल (m) | ghana bādal |
| somber (gloomy) | बदली | badalī |

rain	बारिश (f)	bārish
it's raining	बारिश हो रही है	bārish ho rahī hai
rainy (~ day, weather)	बरसाती	barasātī
to drizzle (vi)	बूंदाबांदी होना	būndābāndī hona

pouring rain	मूसलधार बारिश (f)	mūsaladhār bārish
downpour	मूसलधार बारिश (f)	mūsaladhār bārish
heavy (e.g. ~ rain)	भारी	bhārī
puddle	पोखर (m)	pokhar
to get wet (in rain)	भीगना	bhīgana

fog (mist)	कुहरा (m)	kuhara
foggy	कुहरेदार	kuharedār
snow	बर्फ़ (f)	barf
it's snowing	बर्फ़ पड़ रही है	barf par rahī hai

86. Severe weather. Natural disasters

thunderstorm	गरजवाला तुफ़ान (m)	garajavāla tufān
lightning (~ strike)	बिजली (m)	bijalī
to flash (vi)	चमकना	chamakana

thunder	गरज (m)	garaj
to thunder (vi)	बादल गरजना	bādal garajana
it's thundering	बादल गरज रहा है	bādal garaj raha hai

| hail | ओला (m) | ola |
| it's hailing | ओले पड़ रहे हैं | ole par rahe hain |

| to flood (vt) | बाढ़ आ जाना | bārh ā jāna |
| flood, inundation | बाढ़ (f) | bārh |

earthquake	भूकंप (m)	bhūkamp
tremor, shoke	झटका (m)	jhataka
epicentre	अधिकेंद्र (m)	adhikendr

| eruption | उद्गार (m) | udgār |
| lava | लावा (m) | lāva |

twister	बवंडर (m)	bavandar
tornado	टोर्नेडो (m)	tornedo
typhoon	रतूफ़ान (m)	ratūfān

hurricane	समुद्री तूफ़ान (m)	samudrī tūfān
storm	तूफ़ान (m)	tufān
tsunami	सुनामी (f)	sunāmī

cyclone	चक्रवात (m)	chakravāt
bad weather	ख़राब मौसम (m)	kharāb mausam
fire (accident)	आग (f)	āg
disaster	प्रलय (m)	pralay

meteorite	उल्का पिंड (m)	ulka pind
avalanche	हिमस्खलन (m)	himaskhalan
snowslide	हिमस्खलन (m)	himaskhalan
blizzard	बर्फ़ का तुफ़ान (m)	barf ka tufān
snowstorm	बर्फ़ीला तुफ़ान (m)	barfila tufān

FAUNA

predator	परभक्षी (m)	parabhakshī
tiger	बाघ (m)	bāgh
lion	शेर (m)	sher
wolf	भेड़िया (m)	bheriya
fox	लोमड़ी (f)	lomri
jaguar	जागुआर (m)	jāguār
leopard	तेंदुआ (m)	tendua
cheetah	चीता (m)	chīta
black panther	काला तेंदुआ (m)	kāla tendua
puma	पहाड़ी बिलाव (m)	pahādī bilāv
snow leopard	हिम तेंदुआ (m)	him tendua
lynx	वन बिलाव (m)	van bilāv
coyote	कोयोट (m)	koyot
jackal	गीदड़ (m)	gīdar
hyena	लकड़बग्घा (m)	lakarabaggha

88. Wild animals

animal	जानवर (m)	jānavar
beast (animal)	जानवर (m)	jānavar
squirrel	गिलहरी (f)	gilaharī
hedgehog	कांटा-चूहा (m)	kānta-chūha
hare	खरगोश (m)	kharagosh
rabbit	खरगोश (m)	kharagosh
badger	बिज्जू (m)	bijjū
raccoon	रैकून (m)	raikūn
hamster	हैम्स्टर (m)	haimstar
marmot	मारमोट (m)	māramot
mole	छछूंदर (m)	chhachhūndar
mouse	चूहा (m)	chūha
rat	घूस (m)	ghūs
bat	चमगादड़ (m)	chamagādar
ermine	नेवला (m)	nevala
sable	सेबल (m)	sebal
marten	मारटेन (m)	māraten
weasel	नेवला (m)	nevala
mink	मिंक (m)	mink

beaver	ऊदबिलाव (m)	ūdabilāv
otter	ऊदबिलाव (m)	ūdabilāv
horse	घोड़ा (m)	ghora
moose	मूस (m)	mūs
deer	हिरण (m)	hiran
camel	ऊंट (m)	ūnt
bison	बाइसन (m)	baisan
wisent	जंगली बैल (m)	jangalī bail
buffalo	भैंस (m)	bhains
zebra	ज़ेबरा (m)	zebara
antelope	मृग (f)	mrg
roe deer	मृगनी (f)	mrgnī
fallow deer	चीतल (m)	chītal
chamois	शैमी (f)	shaimī
wild boar	जंगली सुअर (m)	jangalī suār
whale	हेल (f)	hvel
seal	सील (m)	sīl
walrus	वॉलरस (m)	volaras
fur seal	फर सील (f)	far sīl
dolphin	डॉलफ़िन (f)	dolafin
bear	रीछ (m)	rīchh
polar bear	सफ़ेद रीछ (m)	safed rīchh
panda	पांडा (m)	pānda
monkey	बंदर (m)	bandar
chimpanzee	वनमानुष (m)	vanamānush
orangutan	वनमानुष (m)	vanamānush
gorilla	गोरिला (m)	gorila
macaque	अफ़्रीकन लंगूर (m)	afrikan langūr
gibbon	गिब्बन (m)	gibban
elephant	हाथी (m)	hāthī
rhinoceros	गैंडा (m)	gainda
giraffe	जिराफ़ (m)	jirāf
hippopotamus	दरियाई घोड़ा (m)	dariyaī ghora
kangaroo	कंगारू (m)	kangārū
koala (bear)	कोआला (m)	koāla
mongoose	नेवला (m)	nevala
chinchilla	चिनचीला (f)	chinachīla
skunk	स्कंक (m)	skank
porcupine	शल्यक (f)	shalyak

89. Domestic animals

cat	बिल्ली (f)	billī
tomcat	बिल्ला (m)	billa
dog	कुत्ता (m)	kutta

horse	घोड़ा (m)	ghora
stallion (male horse)	घोड़ा (m)	ghora
mare	घोड़ी (f)	ghorī
cow	गाय (f)	gāy
bull	बैल (m)	bail
ox	बैल (m)	bail
sheep (ewe)	भेड़ (f)	bher
ram	भेड़ा (m)	bhera
goat	बकरी (f)	bakarī
billy goat, he-goat	बकरा (m)	bakara
donkey	गधा (m)	gadha
mule	खच्चर (m)	khachchar
pig	सुअर (m)	suar
piglet	घेंटा (m)	ghenta
rabbit	खरगोश (m)	kharagosh
hen (chicken)	मुर्गी (f)	murgī
cock	मुर्गा (m)	murga
duck	बतख़ (f)	battakh
drake	नर बतख़ (m)	nar battakh
goose	हंस (m)	hans
tom turkey, gobbler	नर टर्की (m)	nar tarkī
turkey (hen)	टर्की (f)	tarkī
domestic animals	घरेलू पशु (m pl)	gharelū pashu
tame (e.g. ~ hamster)	पालतू	pālatū
to tame (vt)	पालतू बनाना	pālatū banāna
to breed (vt)	पालना	pālana
farm	खेत (m)	khet
poultry	मुर्गी पालन (f)	murgī pālan
cattle	मवेशी (m)	maveshī
herd (cattle)	पशु समूह (m)	pashu samūh
stable	अस्तबल (m)	astabal
pigsty	सूअरखाना (m)	sūarakhāna
cowshed	गौशाला (f)	goshāla
rabbit hutch	खरगोश का दरबा (m)	kharagosh ka daraba
hen house	मुर्गीखाना (m)	murgīkhāna

90. Birds

bird	चिड़िया (f)	chiriya
pigeon	कबूतर (m)	kabūtar
sparrow	गौरैया (f)	gauraiya
tit (great tit)	टिटरी (f)	titarī
magpie	नीलकण्ठ पक्षी (f)	nīlakanth pakshī
raven	काला कौआ (m)	kāla kaua

crow	कौआ (m)	kaua
jackdaw	कौआ (m)	kaua
rook	कौआ (m)	kaua
duck	बतख़ (f)	battakh
goose	हंस (m)	hans
pheasant	तीतर (m)	tītar
eagle	चील (f)	chīl
hawk	बाज़ (m)	bāz
falcon	बाज़ (m)	bāz
vulture	गिद्ध (m)	giddh
condor (Andean ~)	कॉन्डोर (m)	kondor
swan	राजहंस (m)	rājahans
crane	सारस (m)	sāras
stork	लकलक (m)	lakalak
parrot	तोता (m)	tota
hummingbird	हमिंग बर्ड (f)	haming bard
peacock	मोर (m)	mor
ostrich	शुतुरमुर्ग (m)	shuturamurg
heron	बगुला (m)	bagula
flamingo	फ़्लैमिन्गो (m)	flemingo
pelican	हवासिल (m)	havāsil
nightingale	बुलबुल (m)	bulabul
swallow	अबाबील (f)	abābīl
thrush	मुखव्रण (f)	mukhavran
song thrush	मुखव्रण (f)	mukhavran
blackbird	ब्लैकबर्ड (m)	blaikabard
swift	बतासी (f)	batāsī
lark	भरत (m)	bharat
quail	वर्तक (m)	varttak
woodpecker	कठफोड़ा (m)	kathafora
cuckoo	कोयल (f)	koyal
owl	उल्लू (m)	ullū
eagle owl	गरूड़ उल्लू (m)	garūr ullū
wood grouse	तीतर (m)	tītar
black grouse	काला तीतर (m)	kāla tītar
partridge	चकोर (m)	chakor
starling	तिलिया (f)	tiliya
canary	कनारी (f)	kanārī
hazel grouse	पिंगल तीतर (m)	pingal tītar
chaffinch	फ़िंच (m)	finch
bullfinch	बुलफ़िंच (m)	bulafinch
seagull	गंगा-चिल्ली (f)	ganga-chillī
albatross	अल्बात्रोस (m)	albātros
penguin	पेंगुइन (m)	penguin

91. Fish. Marine animals

bream	ब्रीम (f)	brīm
carp	कार्प (f)	kārp
perch	पर्च (f)	parch
catfish	कैटफ़िश (f)	kaitafish
pike	पाइक (f)	paik
salmon	सैल्मन (f)	sailman
sturgeon	स्टर्जन (f)	starjan
herring	हेरिंग (f)	hering
Atlantic salmon	अटलांटिक सैल्मन (f)	atalāntik sailman
mackerel	माक्रैल (f)	mākrail
flatfish	फ़्लैटफ़िश (f)	flaitafish
zander, pike perch	पाइक पर्च (f)	paik parch
cod	कॉड (f)	kod
tuna	टूना (f)	tūna
trout	ट्राउट (f)	traut
eel	सर्पमीन (f)	sarpamīn
electric ray	विद्युत शंकुश (f)	vidyut shankush
moray eel	मोरे सर्पमीन (f)	more sarpamīn
piranha	पिरान्हा (f)	pirānha
shark	शार्क (f)	shārk
dolphin	डॉलफ़िन (f)	dolafin
whale	ह्वेल (f)	hvel
crab	केकड़ा (m)	kekara
jellyfish	जेली फ़िश (f)	jelī fish
octopus	आक्टोपस (m)	āktopas
starfish	स्टार फ़िश (f)	stār fish
sea urchin	जलसाही (f)	jalasāhī
seahorse	समुद्री घोड़ा (m)	samudrī ghora
oyster	कस्तूरा (m)	kastūra
prawn	झींगा (f)	jhīnga
lobster	लॉब्सटर (m)	lobsatar
spiny lobster	स्पाइनी लॉब्सटर (m)	spainī lobsatar

92. Amphibians. Reptiles

snake	सर्प (m)	sarp
venomous (snake)	विषैला	vishaila
viper	वाइपर (m)	vaipar
cobra	नाग (m)	nāg
python	अजगर (m)	ajagar
boa	अजगर (m)	ajagar
grass snake	साँप (f)	sānp

| rattle snake | रैटल सर्प (m) | raital sarp |
| anaconda | एनाकोन्डा (f) | enākonda |

lizard	छिपकली (f)	chhipakalī
iguana	इग्युएना (m)	igyūena
monitor lizard	मॉनिटर छिपकली (f)	monitar chhipakalī
salamander	सैलामैंडर (m)	sailāmaindar
chameleon	गिरगिट (m)	giragit
scorpion	वृश्चिक (m)	vrshchik

turtle	कछुआ (m)	kachhua
frog	मेंढक (m)	mendhak
toad	भेक (m)	bhek
crocodile	मगर (m)	magar

93. Insects

insect	कीट (m)	kīt
butterfly	तितली (f)	titalī
ant	चींटी (f)	chīntī
fly	मक्खी (f)	makkhī
mosquito	मच्छर (m)	machchhar
beetle	भृंग (m)	bhrng

wasp	हड्डा (m)	hadda
bee	मधुमक्खी (f)	madhumakkhī
bumblebee	भंवरा (m)	bhanvara
gadfly (botfly)	गोमक्खी (f)	gomakkhī

| spider | मकड़ी (f) | makarī |
| spider's web | मकड़ी का जाल (m) | makarī ka jāl |

dragonfly	व्याध-पतंग (m)	vyādh-patang
grasshopper	टिड्डा (m)	tidda
moth (night butterfly)	पतंगा (m)	patanga

cockroach	तिलचट्टा (m)	tilachatta
tick	जुँआ (m)	juna
flea	पिस्सू (m)	pissū
midge	भुनगा (m)	bhunaga

locust	टिड्डी (f)	tiddī
snail	घोंघा (m)	ghongha
cricket	झींगुर (m)	jhīngur
firefly	जुगनू (m)	juganū
ladybird	सोनपंखी (f)	sonapankhī
cockchafer	कोकचाफ़ (m)	kokachāf

leech	जोंक (m)	jok
caterpillar	इल्ली (f)	illī
earthworm	केंचुआ (m)	kenchua
larva	कीटडिंभ (m)	kītadimbh

FLORA

94. Trees

tree	पेड़ (m)	per
deciduous (adj)	पर्णपाती	parnapātī
coniferous (adj)	शंकुधर	shankudhar
evergreen (adj)	सदाबहार	sadābahār
apple tree	सेब वृक्ष (m)	seb vrksh
pear tree	नाशपाती का पेड़ (m)	nāshpātī ka per
cherry tree	चेरी का पेड़ (f)	cherī ka per
plum tree	आलूबुखारे का पेड़ (m)	ālūbukhāre ka per
birch	सनोबर का पेड़ (m)	sanobar ka per
oak	बलूत (m)	balūt
linden tree	लिनडेन वृक्ष (m)	linaden vrksh
aspen	आस्पेन वृक्ष (m)	āspen vrksh
maple	मेपल (m)	mepal
spruce	फर का पेड़ (m)	far ka per
pine	देवदार (m)	devadār
larch	लार्च (m)	lārch
fir tree	फर (m)	far
cedar	देवदर (m)	devadar
poplar	पोप्लर वृक्ष (m)	poplar vrksh
rowan	रोवाण (m)	rovān
willow	विलो (f)	vilo
alder	आल्डर वृक्ष (m)	āldar vrksh
beech	बीच (m)	bīch
elm	एल्म वृक्ष (m)	elm vrksh
ash (tree)	एश-वृक्ष (m)	esh-vrksh
chestnut	चेस्टनट (m)	chestanat
magnolia	मैगनोलिया (f)	maiganoliya
palm tree	ताड़ का पेड़ (m)	tār ka per
cypress	सरो (m)	saro
mangrove	मैनग्रोव (m)	mainagrov
baobab	गोरक्षी (m)	gorakshī
eucalyptus	यूकेलिप्टस (m)	yūkeliptas
sequoia	सेकोइया (f)	sekoiya

95. Shrubs

bush	झाड़ी (f)	jhārī
shrub	झाड़ी (f)	jhārī

| grapevine | अंगूर की बेल (f) | angūr kī bel |
| vineyard | अंगूर का बाग़ (m) | angūr ka bāg |

raspberry bush	रास्पबेरी की झाड़ी (f)	rāspaberī kī jhārī
redcurrant bush	लाल करेंट की झाड़ी (f)	lāl karent kī jhārī
gooseberry bush	गूज़बेरी की झाड़ी (f)	gūzaberī kī jhārī

acacia	ऐकेशिय (m)	aikeshiy
barberry	बारबेरी झाड़ी (f)	bāraberī jhārī
jasmine	चमेली (f)	chamelī

juniper	जूनिपर (m)	jūnipar
rosebush	गुलाब की झाड़ी (f)	gulāb kī jhārī
dog rose	जंगली गुलाब (m)	jangalī gulāb

96. Fruits. Berries

fruit	फल (m)	fal
fruits	फल (m pl)	fal
apple	सेब (m)	seb

| pear | नाशपाती (f) | nāshpātī |
| plum | आलूबुखारा (m) | ālūbukhāra |

strawberry (garden ~)	स्ट्रॉबेरी (f)	stroberī
cherry	चेरी (f)	cherī
grape	अंगूर (m)	angūr

raspberry	रास्पबेरी (f)	rāspaberī
blackcurrant	काली करेंट (f)	kālī karent
redcurrant	लाल करेंट (f)	lāl karent

| gooseberry | गूज़बेरी (f) | gūzaberī |
| cranberry | क्रैनबेरी (f) | krenaberī |

orange	संतरा (m)	santara
tangerine	नारंगी (f)	nārangī
pineapple	अनानास (m)	anānās

| banana | केला (m) | kela |
| date | खजूर (m) | khajūr |

lemon	नींबू (m)	nīmbū
apricot	खूबानी (f)	khūbānī
peach	आड़ू (m)	ārū

| kiwi | चीकू (m) | chīkū |
| grapefruit | ग्रेपफ्रूट (m) | grepafrūt |

berry	बेरी (f)	berī
berries	बेरियां (f pl)	beriyān
cowberry	काओबेरी (f)	kaoberī
wild strawberry	जंगली स्ट्रॉबेरी (f)	jangalī stroberī
bilberry	बिलबेरी (f)	bilaberī

97. Flowers. Plants

flower	फूल (m)	fūl
bouquet (of flowers)	गुलदस्ता (m)	guladasta
rose (flower)	गुलाब (f)	gulāb
tulip	ट्यूलिप (m)	tyūlip
carnation	गुलनार (m)	gulanār
gladiolus	ग्लेडियोलस (m)	glediyolas
cornflower	नीलकूपी (m)	nīlakūpī
harebell	ब्लूबेल (m)	blūbel
dandelion	कुकरौंधा (m)	kukaraundha
camomile	कैमोमाइल (m)	kaimomail
aloe	मुसब्बर (m)	musabbar
cactus	कैक्टस (m)	kaiktas
rubber plant, ficus	रबड़ का पौधा (m)	rabar ka paudha
lily	कुमुदिनी (f)	kumudinī
geranium	जेरानियम (m)	jeraniyam
hyacinth	हायसिंथ (m)	hāyasinth
mimosa	मिमोसा (m)	mimosa
narcissus	नरगिस (f)	naragis
nasturtium	नस्टाशयम (m)	nastāshayam
orchid	आर्किड (m)	ārkid
peony	पियोनी (m)	piyonī
violet	वॉयलेट (m)	voyalet
pansy	पैंज़ी (m pl)	painzī
forget-me-not	फर्गेट मी नाट (m)	fargent mī nāt
daisy	गुलबहार (f)	gulabahār
poppy	खशखाश (m)	khashakhāsh
hemp	भांग (f)	bhāng
mint	पुदीना (m)	pudīna
lily of the valley	कामुदिनी (f)	kāmudinī
snowdrop	सफ़ेद फूल (m)	safed fūl
nettle	बिच्छू बूटी (f)	bichchhū būtī
sorrel	सोरेल (m)	sorel
water lily	कुमुदिनी (f)	kumudinī
fern	फर्न (m)	farn
lichen	शैवाक (m)	shaivāk
conservatory (greenhouse)	शीशाघर (m)	shīshāghar
lawn	घास का मैदान (m)	ghās ka maidān
flowerbed	फुलवारी (f)	fulavārī
plant	पौधा (m)	paudha
grass	घास (f)	ghās
blade of grass	तिनका (m)	tinaka

leaf	पत्ती (f)	pattī
petal	पंखुड़ी (f)	pankharī
stem	डंडी (f)	dandī
tuber	कंद (m)	kand
young plant (shoot)	अंकुर (m)	ankur
thorn	काँटा (m)	kānta
to blossom (vi)	खिलना	khilana
to fade, to wither	मुरझाना	murajhāna
smell (odour)	बू (m)	bū
to cut (flowers)	काटना	kātana
to pick (a flower)	तोड़ना	torana

98. Cereals, grains

grain	दाना (m)	dāna
cereal crops	अनाज की फ़सलें (m pl)	anāj kī fasalen
ear (of barley, etc.)	बाल (f)	bāl
wheat	गेहूं (m)	gehūn
rye	रई (f)	raī
oats	जई (f)	jaī
millet	बाजरा (m)	bājara
barley	जौ (m)	jau
maize	मक्का (m)	makka
rice	चावल (m)	chāval
buckwheat	मोथी (m)	mothī
pea plant	मटर (m)	matar
kidney bean	राजमा (f)	rājama
soya	सोया (m)	soya
lentil	दाल (m)	dāl
beans (pulse crops)	फली (f pl)	falī

COUNTRIES OF THE WORLD

99. Countries. Part 1

Afghanistan	अफ़्ग़ानिस्तान (m)	afagānistān
Albania	अल्बानिया (m)	albāniya
Argentina	अर्जेंटीना (m)	arjentīna
Armenia	आर्मीनिया (m)	ārmīniya
Australia	आस्ट्रेलिया (m)	āstreliya
Austria	ऑस्ट्रिया (m)	ostriya
Azerbaijan	आज़रबाइजान (m)	āzarabaijān
The Bahamas	बहामा (m)	bahāma
Bangladesh	बांग्लादेश (m)	bānglādesh
Belarus	बेलारूस (m)	belārūs
Belgium	बेल्जियम (m)	beljiyam
Bolivia	बोलीविया (m)	bolīviya
Bosnia and Herzegovina	बोस्निया और हर्ज़ेगोविना	bosniya aur harzegovina
Brazil	ब्राज़ील (m)	brāzīl
Bulgaria	बुल्गारिया (m)	bulgāriya
Cambodia	कम्बोडिया (m)	kambodiya
Canada	कनाडा (m)	kanāda
Chile	चिली (m)	chilī
China	चीन (m)	chīn
Colombia	कोलम्बिया (m)	kolambiya
Croatia	क्रोएशिया (m)	kroeshiya
Cuba	क्यूबा (m)	kyūba
Cyprus	साइप्रस (m)	saipras
Czech Republic	चेक गणतंत्र (m)	chek ganatantr
Denmark	डेन्मार्क (m)	denmārk
Dominican Republic	डोमिनिकन रिपब्लिक (m)	dominikan ripablik
Ecuador	इक्वेडोर (m)	ikvedor
Egypt	मिस्र (m)	misr
England	इंग्लैंड (m)	inglaind
Estonia	एस्तोनिया (m)	estoniya
Finland	फ़िनलैंड (m)	finalaind
France	फ़्रांस (m)	frāns
French Polynesia	फ्रेंच पॉलीनेशिया (m)	french polīneshiya
Georgia	जॉर्जिया (m)	jorjiya
Germany	जर्मन (m)	jarman
Ghana	घाना (m)	ghāna
Great Britain	ग्रेट ब्रिटेन (m)	gret briten
Greece	ग्रीस (m)	grīs
Haiti	हाइटी (m)	haitī
Hungary	हंगरी (m)	hangarī

100. Countries. Part 2

Iceland	आयसलैंड (m)	āyasalaind
India	भारत (m)	bhārat
Indonesia	इण्डोनेशिया (m)	indoneshiya
Iran	इरान (m)	irān
Iraq	इराक़ (m)	irāq
Ireland	आयरलैंड (m)	āyaralaind
Israel	इस्रायल (m)	isrāyal
Italy	इटली (m)	italī
Jamaica	जमैका (m)	jamaika
Japan	जापान (m)	jāpān
Jordan	जॉर्डन (m)	jordan
Kazakhstan	कज़ाकस्तान (m)	kazākastān
Kenya	केन्या (m)	kenya
Kirghizia	किर्गीज़िया (m)	kirgīziya
Kuwait	कुवैत (m)	kuvait
Laos	लाओस (m)	laos
Latvia	लाटविया (m)	lātaviya
Lebanon	लेबनान (m)	lebanān
Libya	लीबिया (m)	lībiya
Liechtenstein	लिकटेंस्टीन (m)	likatenstīn
Lithuania	लिथुआनिया (m)	lithuāniya
Luxembourg	लक्ज़मबर्ग (m)	lakzamabarg
North Macedonia	मेसेडोनिया (m)	mesedoniya
Madagascar	मडागास्कार (m)	madāgāskār
Malaysia	मलेशिया (m)	maleshiya
Malta	माल्टा (m)	mālta
Mexico	मेक्सिको (m)	meksiko
Moldova, Moldavia	मोलदोवा (m)	moladova
Monaco	मोनाको (m)	monāko
Mongolia	मंगोलिया (m)	mangoliya
Montenegro	मोंटेनेग्रो (m)	montenegro
Morocco	मोरक्को (m)	morakko
Myanmar	म्यांमर (m)	myāmmar
Namibia	नामीबिया (m)	nāmībiya
Nepal	नेपाल (m)	nepāl
Netherlands	नीदरलैंड्स (m)	nīdaralainds
New Zealand	न्यू ज़ीलैंड (m)	nyū zīlaind
North Korea	उत्तर कोरिया (m)	uttar koriya
Norway	नार्वे (m)	nārve

101. Countries. Part 3

Pakistan	पाकिस्तान (m)	pākistān
Palestine	फिलिस्तीन (m)	filistīn
Panama	पनामा (m)	panāma
Paraguay	परागुआ (m)	parāgua

Peru	पेरू (m)	perū
Poland	पोलैंड (m)	polaind
Portugal	पुर्तगाल (m)	purtagāl
Romania	रोमानिया (m)	romāniya
Russia	रूस (m)	rūs
Saudi Arabia	सऊदी अरब (m)	saūdī arab
Scotland	स्कॉटलैंड (m)	skotalaind
Senegal	सेनेगाल (m)	senegāl
Serbia	सर्बिया (m)	sarbiya
Slovakia	स्लोवाकिया (m)	slovākiya
Slovenia	स्लोवेनिया (m)	sloveniya
South Africa	दक्षिण अफ़्रीका (m)	dakshin afrīka
South Korea	दक्षिण कोरिया (m)	dakshin koriya
Spain	स्पेन (m)	spen
Suriname	सूरीनाम (m)	sūrīnām
Sweden	स्वीडन (m)	svīdan
Switzerland	स्विट्ज़रलैंड (m)	svitzaralaind
Syria	सीरिया (m)	sīriya
Taiwan	ताइवान (m)	taivān
Tajikistan	ताजिकिस्तान (m)	tājikistān
Tanzania	तंज़ानिया (m)	tanzāniya
Tasmania	तास्मानिया (m)	tāsmāniya
Thailand	थाईलैंड (m)	thaīlaind
Tunisia	ट्यूनीसिया (m)	tyunīsiya
Turkey	तुर्की (m)	turkī
Turkmenistan	तुर्कमानिस्तान (m)	turkamānistān
Ukraine	यूक्रेन (m)	yūkren
United Arab Emirates	संयुक्त अरब अमीरात (m)	sanyukt arab amīrāt
United States of America	संयुक्त राज्य अमरीका (m)	sanyukt rājy amarīka
Uruguay	उरुग्वे (m)	urugve
Uzbekistan	उज़्बेकिस्तान (m)	uzbekistān
Vatican City	वेटिकन (m)	vetikan
Venezuela	वेनेज़ुएला (m)	venezuela
Vietnam	वियतनाम (m)	viyatanām
Zanzibar	ज़ैंज़िबार (m)	zainzibār

www.ingramcontent.com/pod-product-compliance
Lightning Source LLC
Chambersburg PA
CBHW070822050426
42452CB00011B/2152